C000196958

# Dirty
# Briefs

# Dirty
# Briefs

MARDLE

To all the hard working and under appreciated criminal barristers, and my much loved and long suffering family.

First published in 2022 by Mardle Books
15 Church Road
London, SW13 9HE
www.mardlebooks.com

Text © 2022 Dave Fendem

Paperback ISBN 9781914451171
eBook ISBN 9781914451683

All rights reserved. No part of this publication may be reproduced in any form or by any means — electronic, mechanical, photocopying, recording, or otherwise — or stored in any retrieval system of any nature without prior written permission from the copyright holders. Dave Fendem has asserted his moral right to be identified as the author of this work in accordance with the Copyright, Designs and Patents Act of 1988.

A CIP catalogue record for this book is available from the British Library.

Every reasonable effort has been made to trace copyright-holders of material reproduced in this book, but if any have been inadvertently overlooked the publishers would be glad to hear from them.

Printed in the UK

10 9 8 7 6 5 4 3 2 1

If David Fendem's misspent youth left him with nothing else, it was an incredible nose for dodginess and mastery in the power of persuasion.

Fendem is a barrister, having practised in the law for over two decades. He represents both prosecution and defence with expertise in crime and mental health work.

Renowned on the legal circuit for his ferocious 'street fighter' style legal battles and smooth talking, he has pulled off results in many highly publicised criminal cases.

# Introduction

I am a criminal barrister and, without sounding too big-headed, a not entirely incompetent one. At least if the measure of competency is the restoration of liberty to those demonstrably guilty of crime, I do all right. Those lucky individuals who have enjoyed my services will tell you that if you find yourself standing next to the shattered window of the local Co-Op with a jemmy in your hand, or you've been caught shagging the neighbours' cat, but you say you're innocent, I am your man.

Throughout my training and career, from the embryonic stages at university, as a trainee, a police station representative, a mental-health-tribunal advocate, magistrate's advocate and, later, a defence and prosecution barrister, I have seen it all. There is little that a person could do in this world that would shock or surprise me by now. I want to share with you some stories of the frankly unbelievable shit that people find themselves in. In doing so I don't limit myself to the punters I have dealt with myself or my own courtroom cases. I shall entertain you with my own personal trials, the highs and, more frequently, the lows as I have attempted to navigate this crazy profession. I shall introduce you to some of my dear colleagues as further examples of the dysfunctional maniacs who make up the criminal bar and in whose hands we entrust the criminal justice system.

These are the raw, unedited reminiscences of a bare-knuckle courtroom advocate.

# Born to Be a Lawyer

R ewind twenty-five years.

My skills in demonstrating to juries that the Arabs really do need to buy sand, the Inuit ice and that an obviously honest witness is not worthy of belief, has not come from idle lying about playing *Fortnite* like the youth of today. On the contrary, the skills of this commendable bullshitter were won on the battlefields of my school and streets of my provincial hometown where, to be frank, I was pretty badly behaved. When one finds oneself regularly in the doggy do, as I did, then knowing how to talk oneself quickly and efficiently out of that doggy do is not just a necessity, but must become a way of life. With the onset of the teen years, and being increasingly led by my penis, things stepped up a gear.

For a somewhat spotty, pigeon-chested and unspectacular individual to be able to persuade a real-life female that it was a good idea to let him anywhere near her pants, let alone inside them, took some real silver-tongued proficiency. Talking myself out of trouble and into bed (and vice versa) made me the lawyer I am today.

A far cry from the liberal parenting values of today mandating the provision of a safe roof above the heads of would-be lovers, my folks made it abundantly clear that their house was not to be used as a 'fucking knocking shop'. Late-night bonking was frowned upon by my parents, so much of my teenage life was spent trying to cover my tracks. My mother once claimed that it wasn't the nature of the act that concerned her so much as the image of the poor girl (for whom she had great sympathy) being exposed to a person as objectionable as me. The origins of my enviable powers of persuasion can, in large part, be traced back to the frivolous dodges employed to distract my eagle-eyed and captious mother from the sweet scent of carefree romance.

My early childhood was spent hanging out in the office of my dad's scrapyard, a place where to be employed, it seemed, a record of previous convictions as long as your arm was required. Take Bill, a booze-soaked, wiry Irishman generously exalted to the post of 'complaints handler'. That was a nice promotion for him having recently 'holidayed' at Her Majesty's pleasure for single-handedly rendering six police officers unconscious as they attempted to load him into a police van one evening. One may ponder the question of what attributes my father had identified in him commensurate with that job, but it's safe to say that the business only rarely received complaints.

Then take the Jones twins, a personable pair of brothers, always willing to lend a hand. Dad told me that they had retired from a lucrative removals business, neglecting to mention that the removals were seldom with the owner's consent.

Despite all of this, there really was honour amongst thieves. It seems for the most part that they all worked hard in the cold, wet and arduous conditions of a waste-paper yard. My dad saw the good in people and liked to offer a chance, regardless of their background. This was my first introduction to people showing themselves capable of hard work and a positive contribution to society when they could otherwise so easily have been written off. I wouldn't go so far as to say that they were entirely law-abiding though. A police car at the yard was a very common occurrence. Frequently, one or more of the employees would be led away in cuffs, hanging out the back window of the police car, screaming to anyone who would listen, 'Phone RT!'

RT was a local defence solicitor who would attend the nick and help these poor arrestees out, for a price. He was the brief of choice for those in the know. His partner TR, a notorious solicitor who could often be seen driving his opulent blue Rolls-Royce through the streets, gained quite a reputation for being a talented lawyer. Between them they commanded most of the business from the local riff-raff and were well-respected figures, trading in a murky underworld, which was at that time totally alien to me, and would remain so until decades later.

Shady scrap-dealing enterprises aside, I was required, like other kids, to go to school. I didn't have an easy time. I was always in some fight or another and my parents were summoned to the school so many times that they almost gave in and took up residence.

If you tell a kid that he is generally a waste of space and that the best he can hope for is a life of crime, then the consequence will often be one of two things: either he will completely give up, impregnate the girl working in the nearby burger van, and spend a career behind the till at a petrol station; or he will work hard to prove a point in making something of himself. In my case, I managed to follow a middle course. I wasn't going to stop savouring the offerings of 'Nat's Baps', but neither was I going to be called a loser. I had a point to make. I worked hard, started to get good results, found my confidence and made it to the local grammar school. Suddenly I had lofty ideas of becoming a medic or an engineer. All now seemed within my grasp.

You may already be getting the impression that I am cut from a different cloth to many barristers. I wasn't educated at one of the top public schools. Unlike lawyers of that ilk, my problems as a youngster extended beyond 'bog washes', casual buggery and similar jolly japes and wheezes. It was being endlessly surrounded by dodgy characters, both friend and foe, that gave me a nose for mischief. I became attuned to sniffing out a ruse, a plan, or a scheme from a good bargepole away. Later in life, as a lawyer, working out what exactly had been going through a client's melon of a head at the time of an alleged incident was the key, not indistinct from Atticus Finch 'wearing a person's skin and walking around in it'. The place to start in all cases was the place where no jury must be allowed to go, an understanding of what truly happened. The more time I spent with these buffoons, the more adept I became in sussing them out, and the more accomplished I became in preventing the *jury* from sussing them out.

A great many of my barrister adversaries, at least in the early days of my crown court practice, were aloof, imperturbably self-possessed, but worse than that, they were totally out of touch with the person they were representing. How can bonking a pig's head in a gentleman's club, or whatever other social activities they enjoyed, possibly provide the tools to appreciate the mind and motivation of the ordinary Joe or to appeal to the values or principles of twelve ordinary citizens who had come to try the case, and required persuading?

My theory on criminal advocacy mirrors the rationale for internet-security firms hiring computer hackers. That fundamental bit of street savvy and mild iniquity needed to shape a defence case into a victory doesn't come from shooting grouse on daddy's estate. It is the Tarquins and the Tobins and the Beazley-Drake-Smyths who stand up to address the jury, speaking Latin, quoting Shakespeare, declaiming Byron and recoiling in disgust at the repugnant notion of a 'Turkish keebarb' who come to grief when they appear on the opposite side of the bench to me. It is those Tarquins and Tobins who, upon lowering their noses, discover to their

5

dismay that their opponent, a country-dwelling ignoramus, has, with cunning, crept up and pulled their trousers down, exposing their rather unimpressively proportioned genitals.

# University Days

People tend to choose university degrees with an eye on their ultimate career. At the very least they will tend to choose a university course which interests them. I loved my mechanics and so a degree in engineering would have been great. I had taken all sciences for A level in the hope that I might even get into medical school. I even managed to get the grades to do just that.

People ask why I chose law. Was it to fight for the rights of the innocent, seek redress for the aggrieved, lift the downtrodden, fight the might of the oppressive state? No, it was in fact because that UCAS book of degrees was so oppressively large that I couldn't face looking in it. My older brother had read law – that was a degree the last time I heard – and so that would do. I just needed to get my nagging mother off my back and return to what was important, which, at that time, happened to be coitus with the hotty from my biology class. I didn't like reading, I didn't like lawyers (my brother included) and I didn't like law. Other than that, four years reading law sounded great!

It may not come as a surprise that I hated uni, or at least the first couple of years. I realised that a parrot, proficient in repeating the names of endless cases would do splendidly in legal exams. Having a somewhat rational, mathematical approach to things, I was frustrated by the inherently contradictory and often irrational fabric of the law. Later in practice I would, as it happened, come to find such inconsistency in approach a friend. It enabled me to start with a preferred destination and then work backwards to find and utilise some law which fitted. Inevitably there would be something of use in the mishmash of pre-existing conflicting legislation. At law school though, it simply contributed to my general aversion to my studies.

I didn't much care for the work, the extensive reading lists or my housemates in either my first or second years. I would travel home as often as possible, avoiding time at uni. That also meant that I didn't work very hard, barely scraping a pass in my first year. That was, however, until one notorious visit back home to my parents', when I accidentally made love to the neighbour.

Had my usual technique when without a key, to scale the front of my house and climb in through my bedroom window in the early hours, not been halted abruptly by a local bobby, then my philandering would have continued largely unabated. Redolent as I was of the Artful Dodger, the rozzer was within his rights to suspect I was in the process of burgling the place and to ignore my piteous pleas against the idea of a street identification involving my parents at 3am. Further revelations that the enterprise had centred around the delicious and lascivious 'friend' of my mother, or 'that tart' as she would thereafter be known to her, caused more shit to hit the fan than I'd ever thought possible. It wasn't the husband's threats that he would hungrily consume my 'bollocks' that concerned me; on the contrary, that act may have been somewhat edifying. It was the promise of a slow and painful death that I felt I could largely do without. I wasn't proud of myself – all right, at eighteen maybe a bit – but my parents, along with most of the neighbourhood, took a dim view of my sexual inconti-nence and complete lack of moral fibre.

For bringing shame on my family, for being chased by neighbours with burning torches and pitchforks, and in the interest of self-preservation, I gave up on my trips home and studied instead, attaining some decent grades for once.

Having made a terrible job of lying my way out of trouble … er … I mean, proposing a scenario of events both consistent with the evidence and my innocence, I also looked deeply inward and vowed never to be caught lying again. I didn't *stop* lying; just resolved to make a better job of it.

By my third year, I was homeless. My previous house-mates had thrown me out for being antisocial. As misfortune would have it, three others had also been thrown out of their respective houses for various indiscretions: substance abuse, sexual profligacy, antisocial behaviour, or all of the above. We all needed a place to stay so we pooled our resources. Regrettably, it also meant living together in our final academic year.

There was no doubting that we all had our own issues, of varying degrees of severity, although the bad behaviour became greater than that of the sum of the individual participants. Our new digs was next door to an executive massage parlour named 'A Touch of Class', which it wasn't, for which reason we dropped the 'Cl' from its name.

The location was chosen at the insistence of one of our number who blew his entire student loan there faster than it took Lady Penelope to sodomise him with a chair leg. Even for us non-participants, the year was one long stream of sex, boozing and quasi-criminality. With the front door destroyed by violence within the first week, icy winds, leaves, and rats were a daily feature, and a Wild West fight between housemates broke all the crockery save a large jam jar which, through necessity, served as my 'do it all' piece of kitchenware for the best part of ten months. Whilst these maniacs could loosely be classed as 'friends', they were the sort of friends who would also delight in the gutting of your room by fire, to use one real-life example.

Having been banned for five months from the student union for an alleged urinal indiscretion, with an additional month to run consecutively for laying down a banana peel on the polished floor of a packed exam room foyer just to see if it was slippery (it was, by the way), my social life was all but over. While my friends partied at the union I did more work, visiting the local boozer, the Sherborn Arms, between times to regale Kelly, the barmaid, with tales of treason upon the high seas. Yes, she sported a tight perm, a lot of leopard-print, large hoop earrings with 'BITCH' written in the middle and a nine-carat, gold belcher chain with a rag-doll pendant, but she was friendly and, importantly, had a pulse.

It was about 2am one night. In my room, front-facing on the upstairs floor, Kelly and I were having a 'cuddle'. From our respective roles as wheelbarrower and wheelbarrowee, Kelly, with her bronzed face pressed against the window, suddenly exclaimed that there was a punch-up in the street. Two of my housemates had returned home from the union drunk and aggressive and were proceeding to needlessly kick the crap out of one of the locals. In fairness it seemed that the 'victim' was also pissed and giving as good as he got, but that was not going to absolve anyone of responsibility.

At around midday on the Tuesday before my final family law exam there was a loud bang on the door. It was a member of the local constabulary who had come to enquire about the alleged assault that had occurred in the street the previous week. One housemate told the officer that he was there, that he had been set upon and was defending himself. My second housemate said that he had been helping out the first housemate and was acting reasonably. I told the officer that I had witnessed the altercation albeit qualified by the protestation that I hadn't been involved. I wished I had said nothing. It transpired that the complainant had made a statement claiming that three men had attacked him and, by our admissions, carefully noted in his pocket book, the officer now had three men, which tied in nicely with the complaint. We were all promptly arrested, thrown into the back of a police car and conveyed to the custody suite of the local nick.

I have never known why custody areas in police stations are called custody 'suites'. The word 'suite' conjures up images of opulence or something with sugar that you put in your mouth for pleasure. I think that they should actually be called 'custody shitholes'. This was my first experience of one. Passing through a cage at the back of the police station we were frog-marched to the designated custody sergeant, a barrel of a man who sat behind a desk in the foyer area, chicken tikka kebab roll in one hand, pen in the other and with a smacked-arse face of utter contempt. We were told that we had the right to a lawyer, for someone to be told where we were, and we could make a phone call if we liked. I chose to call my dad. I knew it wasn't going to be a call enthusiastically received. I also knew that the fact that I was entirely innocent would make not one jot of difference. My father knew me and, in his mind, whatever it was they were saying I had done, I almost certainly had done. His helpful advice, 'to get myself out of the shit on my own', peppered with a few 'fucks' and 'stupid twats', before he hung up, did little to quell my anxiety.

We were relieved of belts, keys and money. Presumably the officer took my keys so that I couldn't unlock the cell door and run away and my belt so that I couldn't hang myself, but it didn't seem as if there would be much opportunity to spend my money if I'm honest. All three of us were then escorted around the corner and put in a cell, awaiting the arrival of the duty solicitor.

When an accused person is arrested, he has the right to consult a solicitor. Ordinarily the police wish to conduct a tape-recorded interview in which they put the allegation to the accused person and invite answers. If a solicitor has been requested, he or she usually sits in on the interview too, having given advice to their client beforehand as to the best thing to do in the interview and ensuring that the questioning is appropriate and fair. Solicitors secretly, sometimes not so secretly, hope that their client gets charged with an offence, in other words that they are required to attend court and the case proceeds beyond the police-station stage. Lawyers need court cases. That is how they earn a living.

The old hands of the criminal fraternity usually have a favoured brief or firm that they like to use, remember RT and the yard employees? If you had a name for the brief and their firm, the sergeant would phone up the 24-hour contact number of the law firm and somebody would be sent down. Representation is free, paid for by the state. For those, like us, who didn't have our own solicitors, the duty solicitor is there to help. The duty solicitor is nothing to do with the police; most criminal solicitors are also duty solicitors. To become one, additional qualifications are needed.

Duty solicitors are admitted to a rota and when their name comes up, work is referred to them by an independent call centre contacted by the police. A similar scheme operates at the magistrates' court for those defendants who do not have legal representation.

Solicitors are busy people. A duty solicitor may have numerous suspects to deal with at the same time, often at different police stations. They need to travel to the station, gain access, speak to the officer about the evidence, speak to their client about his case, advise the client and then sit in on a police interview.

To the police the brief is, generally speaking, a colossal pain in the arse. The brief and the police usually rub along okay because, like Brussels sprouts on your Christmas dinner plate, whilst you would love to drop-kick them out of the nearest window, you would get an almighty bollocking from someone if you did. Briefs are part of the deal. When all is said and done, everyone has their job to do; everyone would rather be at home in bed with the missus or hubby (or with someone else's missus or hubby), or, frankly, anywhere other than the shitty custody suite. Both parties have the power to make the life of the other needlessly harder if so inclined. Sometimes it gets nasty; usually it doesn't.

The solicitor will inevitably delay proceedings and prevent, as far as they are able to, the police from gathering evidence against their client. The police gather evidence, the brief opposes it. That is clearly not a good springboard for happy bedfellows. Little sleep is lost by the police then should they drag their heels or delay access of the solicitor to the custody area until they have finished their coffee, pie, poo or whatever else they deem more edifying.

It may be apparent, therefore, that a suspect can be left waiting in a cell for hours. When I later started my career in the law and began to attend police stations to represent detainees, often it would all kick off because of hours spent alone in the confines of that dreadful cell. Whilst improper, it is often remarked by the clientele that the police are occasionally inclined to make a suspect acutely aware of the delay a request for a solicitor can cause and that if that request is not made, they may be out in a jiffy, perhaps with bail. The police know, of course, that the lawyer's aim of maintaining an accused's innocent status, begins in the police station. The outcome of cases can turn entirely on what work the brief does at this early, but crucial, stage.

Police cells are grim places to find oneself, and ours was no exception. A big, heavy, steel door marks the entrance to a whitewashed, eight-by-six-foot room lit by a single, fluorescent bulb. Some have a stainless-steel toilet without a toilet seat, and there is a thin, blue, easy-wipe mattress on a wooden bench. Police cells are also, almost without exception, either very cold or boiling hot, not that that bothers the occasional silverfish creepy-crawly that will be seen oscillating across the floor. If you are lucky, you may be thrown a scratchy grey blanket made from some strange, recycled material and a copy of the police codes of practice, which, as dull as they may sound, are as exciting as a porno mag to a cub scout after the previous five hours

15

staring at a blank wall. Expect to be sat in there for a very long time. Initially, the police can detain you for up to twenty-four hours, but in some circumstances, this can be extended to seventy-two hours. At the very least, you can expect to be detained until after the recorded interview and until a decision has been made to charge you or not.

My experience of the cell seemed to last a lifetime. The hours rolled by and I became increasingly anxious, primarily because my exam, for which I had done no revision, was the next day. Crying, pleading and banging on the door evoked precisely zero sympathy. Eventually the duty solicitor showed up, a man in his late twenties – pale, a bit sweaty and of a somewhat nervous disposition. He described himself as 'the young Perry Mason'. I was thinking more village idiot. Later court appearances did not dissuade me from the view that the self-proclaimed 'young Perry Mason' was, in fact, a nob. Here in the cop shop, though, I wasn't well placed to quibble, and he did an adequate enough job. He told me to answer the police questions, which I did, regaling the uninterested interrogators with stories of alibis and barmaids with all the bells and whistles, not that they were remotely persuaded. We were all charged with malicious wounding, given a court date, bailed and then booted out at 4am. I pretty much flunked my exam five hours later before phoning my parents to break the good news of the legal apocalypse.

My impending practical legal experience as a defendant in the magistrates' court was scheduled for two weeks hence.

The idea behind a magistrates' court is to dispense summary justice in a cost-efficient way. The court is presided over by a legally-qualified 'district judge' or up to three lay magistrates, who are simply volunteers, but who have the benefit of a qualified legal advisor. A magistrates' court will try crimes of a less serious nature to those heard in a crown court, and there are some crimes that can only be tried in a magistrates' court. Examples of these so-called 'summary only offences' include minor criminal damage, common assault, taking a car without consent and some road-traffic offences. Other crimes can be heard in either a magistrate's court or a crown court. These are known in the trade as 'either way' offences. Examples include theft, assault occasioning actual bodily harm and malicious wounding. Finally, there are some crimes that can be heard only in a crown court: murder, robbery and rape are examples. These are known as 'indictable only' crimes.

All cases begin in a magistrates' court and at the first hearing the court will inquire of the defendants whether they are guilty or not guilty of the charges. If a defendant pleads guilty then the court will decide if it is able to pass sentence. Summary matters, subject to limited exceptions, stay in the magistrates' court for sentence. Similarly, the more serious 'indictable only' cases always get sent to a crown court. For an 'either way' offence, i.e., one that could potentially be heard either in a magistrates' or a crown court, the court must decide on the most appropriate venue. Ordinarily, a sentence of six months' imprisonment is the ceiling for a magistrates' court; if it is felt that the offence warrants greater punishment than six months, the case will be committed to a crown court for sentencing

If a defendant pleads not guilty then a similar procedure takes place for the 'either way' offences. The court must, with reference to a number of factors, which include sentencing powers and the predicted complexity of the case, decide upon the most appropriate court, in other words whether to keep the case in the magistrates' court or send it to a crown court for trial. Even if the court considers that it is able to retain the case, the defendant may choose to be tried before a jury in a crown court.

If the defendant has been charged with something serious, he will almost certainly be represented by a solicitor. If he doesn't have much money, then the state, by means of legal aid, will cover the reasonable costs of his representation, although the word 'reasonable' when it comes to state funding is itself a matter of conjecture.

Whether to persuade a magistrates' court to try a case or to try to secure a crown-court trial for an 'either way' offence is often a tactically important decision for the defence solicitor to make with his client. A magistrates' court has limited sentencing powers and is unaccustomed to handing out heavy sentences. If the defendant is convicted, he may benefit from that. A crown-court judge, by contrast, often with years of experience of handing out lengthy prison sentences may think that four years in the clink is akin to being given a balloon and a ride on the tea cups. Moreover, if a defendant is convicted and the crown-court judge thinks that the expense and trouble of a crown-court trial was a total waste, the obvious result is an unpropitious environment in which to plead for a lenient sentence.

Weighed against all this is the bare fact that a defendant is many times more likely to get off with a jury than with a lay bench of magistrates or a district judge. There are a number of reasons for this. District judges, for example, are case-hardened. They have heard all of the excuses many times before. It is the boy-who-cried-wolf syndrome. The one time a wolf genuinely has tried to eat the defendant, or to indulge in other bestial acts, the defendant won't be believed by the judge. Furthermore, in a crown court a prosecutor would need to convince twelve jurors of a defendant's guilt to secure a conviction, a much more challenging task than convincing a single judge or three magistrates..

In the event that a magistrates' court *does* try a case, a defendant may think that he or she is better off with magistrates than with a district judge, as the former are volunteers, non-legal members of the public. That may sometimes be the case. Some magistrates are empathetic, open-minded and mentally agile. Sadly, many are not. Too many that I later encountered in my career appeared to be people who felt that their self-proclaimed liberalism and empathy was best articulated with a robust meting out of justice redolent of the methods of Ghengis Khan. Whilst many are switched on, far too many magistrates tend not to be known for their cerebral agility, preferring to eschew the fundamental presumption of innocence prescribed by the law in favour of an attitude of 'no smoke without fire'. The 'you wouldn't be here if you hadn't done something wrong' approach combined with almost unthinking acceptance of police evidence, and that of any other witnesses for the prosecution guarantees a sticky wicket for the defendant. Your stereotypical magistrate appears to believe that a robust approach is needed to deal with villainy and that 'leniency' is just a lunch ticket to more crime. They, too, will become case-hardened if they sit for extended periods of time.

To make matters worse, a magistrate will at times be confronted by the palpable derision of the lawyers and legal advisers alike, who might regard them as idiots and whose lack of respect is only thinly veiled with obsequious politeness. The reactionary display of strength, which, in the absence of any power to hang the arrogant lawyer by the neck until dead, tends to manifest itself in the form of a conviction for the poor defendant. In addition, magistrates make decisions on the law as well as on the facts, unlike a judge and jury, where the jury decides on the facts of a case and the judge rules on the law. Of course, if the magistrates make a legal ruling excluding evidence prejudicial to the defence, for example a previous conviction, then all they need to do is put it out of their minds so as not to prejudice their verdicts. And pigs might fly.

You will rarely see a barrister in the magistrates' court other than baby ones, cutting their teeth, finding their feet and earning their wings. Fuck-ups are better made in a magistrates' court than in a crown court where the stakes are higher. For those who like to dress up in wigs and gowns, the crown court is the place to be seen. In the magistrates' court, rules of evidence go out of the window, magistrates get prejudiced by hearing things that should never be said, and the prosecutors are, for the most part, buffoons.

If you are genuinely serious about getting an acquittal, avoid the magistrates' court if you can. There are, of course, exceptions, but by adopting 'I am fucked if these guys try me' as a mantra *ab initio*, from the beginning, you won't go far wrong.

# Trial of the Coburn Three

There was nothing at all funny about us having to attend court other than the fact that on each appearance the accused were required to announce their home addresses for the court record, and one of our number lived at 'The Cock Hotel'.

We all pleaded not guilty at our first appearance in the magistrates' court. It appeared that my two friends wished to aver reasonable self-defence while my defence was alibi. The venue for the trial was not considered at that time as I was keen to instruct a new solicitor and to leave the young Perry Mason to continue his orational mastery on behalf of my two associates.

Solicitors and barristers are both lawyers, but there is a division of function between them. Solicitors are busy people, often with filing cabinets full of case files. They represent suspects day and night at police stations, interview witnesses, instruct experts and advise their clients as to all aspects of their case. Attendance at the magistrates' court is a central part of their daily ritual where they conduct every type of hearing, including trials. They are much more hands-on with the defendants than barristers.

Should matters proceed to the crown court, this is where barristers get involved. If cases need prosecuting, then the Crown Prosecution Service will select a barrister from an approved list. For defence cases, the defence solicitor will choose a barrister and send through a 'brief' to his or her chambers. The brief contains the case papers with a note from the solicitor giving some general information as to the defence case, the solicitor's view on the case and some of the history of proceedings. Traditionally, the brief and papers were wrapped up in string and tied with a bow – pink for defence work and white for prosecution – but now everything is digital. Gone are the days of paper and with it those of misplacing briefs and making excuses – thankfully. A barrister's toolkit is now simply an iPad.

The barrister advises the solicitor with regard to case preparation, but his or her primary job is to do the talking in court. All of the pre-trial hearings and ultimately the trial itself are handled by the barrister.

In my hunt for a solicitor suitably skilled to help me out of the fine mess in which I had found myself, somebody passed me the details of a man in my university town reputed to be one of the best in the game. With the address of the offices scribbled on a crumpled piece of paper, I made my way down to a part of town where I had never before ventured. A rough part of the town I might suggest. The offices were not what I had imagined from sitting in the lecture theatres surrounded by civil lawyers hailing from multi-million-pound glass-fronted modernity. This was a completely different prospect altogether.

Found within a depressing, concrete, 1970s' office block, their name was etched on a small card in a plastic intercom. The reception area on the third floor was the only thing to suggest their existence. Buzzed past a desk protected by reinforced glass, clearly designed to protect against villainy, I was invited into a room for my first meeting. Above the sea of haphazardly strewn papers and to the side of the wooden penholder that rose like a mast from its thief-proof bolted base, I spotted my lawyer gazing out of the window from his knackered old office chair. Nicotine-stained wallpaper adorned with old practising certificates and a twig where a yukka plant had once grown provided a fitting backdrop to his decidedly unenthusiastic appearance.

I could tell that the fifty-something man, with a deeply furrowed face and a calm aura, seated in front of a sagging Venetian blind had shaken hands with more criminals than I had had hot meals. He introduced himself, revealing himself to be a homegrown Welshman, lit a fag before offering me one and then picked up some paperwork from near the top of a pile which I assumed must have been related to my case.

What struck me most about this man as we spoke was his incredible mastery of ventriloquism. When he asked for my account of events, although I seemed to be talking, the words that came out of my mouth did not seem to be mine. He was, in effect, a translator of the incoherent and ill-informed, a mystical turd polisher if you will, effortlessly converting clumsy inarticulacy into something almost plausible.

In discussing the events of that fateful evening, I tried to let him know that I had been wearing 'boxer shorts', but choked on the words. All I could say was 'underpants'. I tried to explain how in the later stages of the event I had 'split things up', but the word 'dissipate' materialised without my lips even moving. 'Angry' was voiced as 'distressed', 'fucking the barmaid' as 'romantic embrace'. Without my realising it, the demonstrably questionable was beginning to sound reasonable, and I didn't even feel a thing.

It was around this time that I smugly showed off a bit of knowledge of crown court and magistrates practice learned from my crime lectures, and told him of my resolve to opt for a crown court trial regardless of whether or not the magistrates accepted jurisdiction. I knew of the higher acquittal rates in the crown court and fancied a bit of that, if he wouldn't mind? Looking at me inquisitively for a moment, he insincerely applauded my hard-earned education.

'Each day,' he said, 'a local Welshman in this town will collect an upturned road cone from his front garden. The local *Heddlu* (policeman) will repatriate a "workmen in the road" sign three miles from the student halls of residence to the roadworks from where it had come. Mrs Jones will hose the piss from her petunias, Mr Evans will swill the vomit from his doorstep, size-nine dents will be beaten out of Mr Smith's car roof.'

He lit another fag, taking a large drag before observing in a comforting, avuncular tone of voice, 'You are one of those twats.' There then followed a pause which I felt was questionably too long for him to make the qualification...

'As far as a jury might be concerned.'

He continued.

'Trial by jury is your choice, but the pool of jurors is drawn from the local community. It might serve you well to consider that a malevolent, torch-waving, English-student-hating, lynch mob of three, is better than one of twelve.'

I wondered to what extent the instantaneous loosening of my bowels was actually detectable.

'Fag?'

He tossed his packet of B&H across the desk but I politely declined.

After some quiet reflection, I felt I might swerve the whole trial-by-jury thing after all and politely invited him to try to keep the case in the magistrates' court. The trial date preceded my graduation by a day or two and I was now more uncertain than ever whether I would be observing my ceremony through a cell window of the local prison or seated, in robes and mortar board, next to my parents, gran and peers. There was a lot at stake, possibly my entire career, and I was terrified.

On the day of the trial, the complainant failed to attend court to testify against us. Everybody knew that the absence of a complainant in a case like this greatly weakens the prosecution case, so this was significant. The prosecution applied to adjourn the case in order to find him and bring him to court, but my solicitor opposed this, doing so in such a magnificently courteous and eloquent way that I was truly wowed. Even the chairwoman of the court was mesmerised by him, the cheeky sparkle in his eyes and seductive address having her all a flutter.

Finding in favour of the defence, the magistrates retired briefly to allow the prosecution to discuss their next move with the defence. The second they left the room, that alluring and genteel man who had moments before charmed the birds from the trees, was reborn as a bloodthirsty hit-man.

Thinking that she could proceed with the case against us in any event because other witnesses had seen the fight, the prosecutor was robustly disabused of the idea. It was pointed out to her that, whilst having observed the injuries post altercation, other witnesses could not attest to the injuries having not been present before the altercation. The evidence would be just as consistent with the possibility, for example, that the complainant had fallen over in the park, injuring himself on his way home, as it would with the suggestion that he had had seven bells kicked out of him by three drunken louts. The prosecution would be unable to prove what had caused the injuries.

Conceding the point, the prosecution suggested that they could proceed then on a simple common assault. 'No,' said my solicitor, 'one can consent to common assault and, in the absence of testimony from the complainant to the contrary, the prosecution would be unable to prove that this was anything other than a consensual fight, the prosecution of course bearing the burden of proof.'

As the trial was not going to be adjourned to allow the prosecution to find the witness, and essential elements of any offence could not be proved in his absence, the prosecution would have to throw in the towel and concede to the entering of not guilty verdicts for all three of us. And so it was. Genius.

It wasn't just the very intelligent logic that my solicitor deployed in bringing about our acquittals that impressed me so much, but also the way in which he undid the prosecutor with both precision and cunning in equal measure. In stark contrast to his courtroom manner before the bench, he switched colours like a chameleon when the climate called for it, exchanging seduction for ruthlessness at the flick of a switch. The prosecutor's lack of confidence couldn't be hidden from a hunter of this calibre and he efficiently deployed the weapons in his armoury to deliver a killer blow. He had one goal, the one shared by all criminal defence lawyers, to get the best result for his client, and in pursuit of that goal he revealed himself to be a true master. The young Perry Mason, who had remained quiet throughout the proceedings, looked on in admiration, as did we all.

I walked away a free man, and with the valuable experience of having seen a brilliant lawyer in action when my own arse was on the line. I thanked him profusely and, for his part, he expressed relief that justice had prevailed, shortly before advising me not to do it again!

I have never forgotten this experience when on so many occasions in my own career I witnessed the same fear in the eyes of those I represented, and whose turds I came to polish.

# London Calling

Whereas my law-student friends were all talking about the 'magic circle' civil firms in the City of London and how the fastest way to orgasm for them would be to be offered a training contract there, I questioned whether working day and night in an office pushing paper around when answerable to some loathsome swinging dick was really my platter of Peshawaris. Doubtless I would encounter wealth, buy expensive drinks in flash bars, maybe even drive a Porsche, but I would also inevitably find myself out of a job on account of headbutting a colleague for his insufferable arrogance. I knew lawyers of that ilk and didn't care much to follow the familiar path of the 'successful' civil practitioner: to end up fat, bald and asleep at my desk while my wife sucked off her salsa teacher.

Crime was the route for me, not because I cared one iota for the downtrodden of society, for justice or the rule of law generally, but because crime looked like fun and civil looked utterly shite, to use the 'lingua franca'. It was this reasoning that led me to apply for a solicitor-training contract at a large, criminal-law firm in London.

Rolling up for my interview in my best attire, I found it curious that the big boss who interviewed me was not interested in my examination results, whether I had won mooting competitions, or spent a year doing aid relief work in Uganda. He wanted to know: a) was I tough; b) if I had a strong stomach for smelly people; and c) how hard I could work when sleep-deprived. That was it.

I don't know whether it was something I *had* said, something I hadn't said or on account of being a persistent pest that I was offered a training contract. I say I was 'offered a training contract', but I would in fact be employed as a 'pre-trainee'. The idea was that I would become police-station qualified at which point my training contract would begin. That way, the firm could pay me a pittance for as long as possible while simultaneously creaming in a fortune from my police-station representations and court clerking. Despite the title 'pre-trainee' sounding important, in truth, when compared with a 'trainee solicitor', it was as 'pre-ejaculate' compares to 'ejaculate': full of promise but entirely useless.

Presently, it was soon apparent that I was regarded as anything but important by the solicitors for whom I, and the other nine in the same position at the firm, were worked to oblivion for little cash or respect.

Despite what I have said of them, the 'pre-trainees' were not actually at the bottom of the office hierarchy. That place was reserved for the 'clerks' whose job it was to attend court hearings with the barristers and take notes. Not that these subtleties in status, albeit important to us, made any difference to our accommodation. The clerks, pre-trainees, and trainees all worked out of an intolerably unventilated and dark basement annex to the offices, well out of the way of anyone of any actual standing. If you found yourself in the higher echelons of the inconsequential, in other words, as a trainee solicitor assigned to work on behalf of a partner in the firm, then you might be promoted into a shared office on the first floor. You were still treated with utter contempt, but at least had a window from which to jump.

As is the case in many workplaces, it was generally assumed a good idea to brown-nose and, as the boss put it, with no hint of an implied threat of firing, to 'make yourself indispensable'. That was the only way to move up the ranks. It was also once remarked by the same boss that when he said 'the law has its perks', he did not have in mind casual embraces with the legal secretaries, neither when he cordially invited a young employee to photocopy documents until 2am did he expect the invitation to be politely declined. For failing to meet his expectations on both fronts, habitually, I was condemned to the annex for at least six months longer than I should have been, and, by the time I eventually climbed the stairs to the first floor as a fully-fledged trainee I was more than ready (read, 'pissed off').

Each partner in the firm was assigned a trainee, or more usually two, and a row of rooms on the first floor were occupied by a pair each. I was greeted at my new desk by

31

my fellow trainee James, a year my senior and with whom I would work for one of the more challenging partners. He was a chancer, a bullshitter and a laggard, but, in spite of this, he became one of my very great friends. The partner for whom we worked was endlessly stressed and overworked and it was our job to take on as much of her casework as possible around attending police stations. There was no actual in-house training to speak of; you learnt on the job and prayed that any inevitable fuck-ups could be covered up, attributed to someone else (or a combination of both) or would be of insufficient gravity to result in the loss of your job.

The pressure was enormous. The phone rang relentlessly. Every five minutes, the partner would enter the room clutching yet another beaten-up file with thousands of documents requiring work, be it legal arguments, proofs of evidence, synopses, schedules, expert instruction, funding applications, briefs to counsel and all the rest of it. Often the work needed to have been done weeks before and the bollockings would always land on the head of the trainees who would never, ever have the time to be on top of things. I have never known a criminal solicitor to refuse a case. Cases mean money and the pattern was always the same. The solicitor took on every case available in order to hit her costs target and get her bonus. The fact that she lacked any capacity for more cases meaning that work on them would not get done on time was of 'nil desperandum'; there were trainees to be scapegoated for that.

And then there were the police stations. My job as a pre-trainee, and later trainee-solicitor, mainly encompassed police-station representations and work on the case files. Once qualified for police stations, I, like the other trainees, would attend police stations round the clock in the roughest parts of London. With a twenty-four-hour police station representation service, as is the norm for any criminal firm of solicitors, the 'bleep' phone was always active. The solicitors, of course, had better things to do than get out of bed at 3.24am to bail Jayden Taylor out of Walworth nick; that job fell squarely on the shoulders of the trainees.

The trainees all worked on an internal rota and when your name was up, you were passed the cheap mobile phone which was to ruin your life for the next twenty-four hours. It was a shit-bomb. In fact, I am sure that I speak for all of my fellow tortured and damned when I say, I would rather have been passed a real-life shit bomb, guaranteed to explode, cover me in excrement and take an arm off, than that awful phone. It promised broken sleep, if any at all, and assured a greater brain-drain than any other aspect of legal practice.

A lawyer's work in the police station can mean the difference between conviction or acquittal at trial and you never know what case you might encounter. You will find yourself in a generally unwelcoming police environment late at night, on your own, and facing a task which demands inquisitorial application, legal knowledge at your fingertips, and the ability to think fast. At twenty-one, advising a local gang member what to do in a police station in respect of a high-profile murder allegation, for example, is a big responsibility for a kid not long out of university. Such situations were not the exception.

Still, at least you were reassured not to be daunted if you were ever faced with the seemingly insurmountable. The partners in the firm implored you to phone a solicitor at any time of the day or night if you needed help with a legal, practical or even a personal question whilst there. They would hurriedly answer their phone, cheerily pop up out of bed and enthusiastically go to work in the early hours of the morning, doing whatever they could to hold your hand and guide you through… yeah, whatever, mate!

What with police stations being thrown into the mix, which were themselves like a sausage factory, it is little wonder that the trainees relied on caffeine and power-naps in the conference room to compensate for sleep deprivation.

And it wasn't as if the abundance of wildflower meadows could ease one's troubled mind. One does not find criminal solicitors' offices located in the plush parts of town. They are located near the client base. The view out of my office window was of high-rise flats, a clutch of dodgy fried-chicken shops, an iffy-looking butcher, a second-hand sofa shop advertising 'incredible bargains', and various independent convenience stores stocking a pretty dismal array of goods. The tube rumbled past every five minutes, making the whole building shake. The noise of police sirens was continuous, occasionally interspersed with the dulcet thuds of street violence and, on one occasion, the blood-curdling cries of a person butchered with a machete right outside my window. I am sure you get the picture.

Training took two years and survival was the goal. The everyday experience of the trainee was of significant levels of trouble and anxiety; judicious exercise of communication skills was called for, along with creativity with the facts and economy with the truth. Yet more years of talking my way out of my own difficulties under pressure did more to turn me into a successful courtroom advocate than any case which I worked on, or statute that I read.

# Flattery Gets You Everywhere, Flatulence Nowhere

The partner came in clutching two huge paper files under her arm, pretty much your standard daily occurrence. It was still early in my training and so I had little clue what I was doing. I was told that this was the case of M and that I was to collect three more boxes of papers from the partner's room.

As was becoming all too frequent, James glanced over from his desk opposite mine, grinned treacherously, and then looked down so as not to meet the eyes of the partner as she stomped in with further instructions. This always meant the same thing. The case was impenetrably complex, the partner was unable to get on top of it and had given it to James, James had procrastinated and kicked the file about the floor of the office for a month, and now, we were all in the shit. I correct that: it was I that was now in the shit, the excrement ball having passed into my hands last. Now, all of the failings to date would be attributable to me.

They may tell you that it is all swings and roundabouts, but they fail to mention that the partner hangs onto the swings; you, meanwhile, are locked to the roundabout. And, to take the playground-equipment metaphor to its fullest conclusion, James will be found rocking on the spring-mounted plastic chicken as the world passes him by. Resigned to my fate, I began to read up on the case.

Mr M had been charged with a pornography offence, while employed as an IT manager. A somewhat dysphoric and rotund character, he habitually consumed raw broccoli out of a tupperware box. Not, it seemed, due to some peculiar predilection for the vegetable, but rather with the hostile intention of generating volcanic volumes of flatulence to annoy his neighbours. With these air biscuits, he would torment, beleaguer and possibly even asphyxiate his colleagues whom, as may be apparent, he disliked intensely. Responding, as any self-respecting recipient of Mr M's filthy onslaught might, they grassed him up to the authorities for illegal porn.

The case was simple enough on its facts. Mr M had been found with about twenty images on his computer which were prohibited. The complexity and voluminous documentation generated during the forensic investigation of his phone and computers by the police related less to these images per se, and more to the unbounded scale of his 'hobby'.

The first thing to do was to get Mr M into the office and find out what he had to say for himself. He told me that he was something of a porn connoisseur, having devoured many hundreds of thousands of images of legitimate pornography in the past. The prohibited images, when viewed against his comprehensive collection, amounted to such a tiny percentage that their existence could be accounted for by inadvertent downloading. Acknowledging that the chances of inadvertent downloading were small in a single sitting, when talking massive amounts of images over a protracted period, the chance of unintended illegal images materialising became greater. At least that was the argument. It was certainly true, even at a cursory glance, that the sheer volume of legal pornography was suggestive of an interest in mature women rather than the subject of the images that formed the charge. To make or possess a prohibited image on one's computer, according to the law, that person must have knowledge of it. Mr M denied knowledge of the prohibited images, and that was his defence.

During the course of an investigation the police must retain all potentially relevant material that they gather, whether or not they use it all as part of their case. The rationale behind this is that there may be something languishing in it that could potentially undermine the case for the prosecution or assist the defence case. The material has to be reviewed and logged. Evidence not used as part of the prosecution's case is known in the trade, perhaps unsurprisingly, as 'unused material'. I called up the police officer in charge of the case and arranged to view the 'unused material' as I needed to see whether there was anything that might assist the defence case before instructing a computer expert.

Ordinarily, copies of the unused material would be sent over, however the officer told me that it was not expedient to do so and I would need to come down to the station, which is what I did. When I got there, I understood why copies hadn't been sent over. The officer unlocked a door to a room about the size of a small bungalow and my eyes were met with distasteful photographs of undressed ladies from floor to ceiling, save for a narrow walkway crafted between what appeared to be pornography's answer to the North Face of the Eiger. No Postman Pat van in the world was going to be able to handle delivery of that lot.

Now, I had a job to do, and one to be undertaken solemnly, but nobody could pretend that this was anything other than a 'Gus and Franker's' paradise, not that I would regard myself as that, you must understand. But you know how things are. It would be paltering with the truth to say that the scene in Willy Wonka, the one where the kids are ushered into the room where everything is made of sweets and there is a river of chocolate, didn't spring to mind. As the stone was rolled back on this Aladdin's cave of grott and the sunlight peeped cheerily through to illuminate the jewels within I could almost hear the theme tune 'dar dar dee, dar dar dee, dar dar dee dee dee dee dee dee dee dar'. I was even waiting for the police officer to clutch his head with both hands and cry out, 'Augustus, no! Don't touch the chocolate, you filthy little bastard!'

Please, before you start with your pious, 'Don't tell me this guy is regaling us with his titillation on the back of his client's sordid exploits', save your sanctimony. There was no illegal pornography there; that stuff was locked away elsewhere, seized as part of the case. Consistent with my client's instructions, this was nothing more than a few million copies of good, old-fashioned cliterature, and this was a good day. I make no apologies. And for all your doubtless disappointment in my moral fabric, you will be buoyed to learn that, by the end of it, I didn't just leave with mild blindness and hairy palms, but with evidence that might just exonerate my client. I made my way back to the office with a large box of 'evidence', not without the scenario having played out in my mind of stumbling on the bus and the box bursting open at the feet of a pensioner with a shopping wheelie. I would, of course, have had a legitimate argument for my possession of it, but the image of the Caprice lookalike and the 'one with the sheep' may have taken a little more explaining.

Dragging myself back to the task, the file paths printed on the top of some of the images corresponded with the idea that the illegal images were linked and downloaded inadvertently as part of a bulk download. I also discovered that some 'unused material' had not been logged and indeed had been lost by the police. This offended the law and had the potential to support a stay of proceedings on the back of an artful legal argument about fair trials, and that sort of jazz. In the end I didn't need to make that legal argument, or even instruct the barrister as to my findings. I wrote to the Crown Prosecution Service threatening to create trouble over their neglect of potentially important material and their response was to fall on their sword and drop the case. The final job was to clear up the paperwork, in furtherance of which I queried with the boss what should be done with the redundant box of porn that now languished on my office floor.

'Give it to Jonny, the office lad,' she said.

Jonny was the odd-job guy at the firm, tasked with the storage and disposal of files and generally fixing shit that went wrong. He was also 'a little strange', not to mention a reputed 'pencil squeezer'. I had my reservations, obviously, but who was I to point out to the boss the conspicuous perils? I presented the box to Jonny with no word of instruction other than to have a happy Christmas (it was April), and departed. I then called the client to tell him the good news. I thought about warning him to be more careful with who he pointed his foul arse at next time but considered that I was paid to be his lawyer and not the voice of his conscience. That would be extra.

# Death is Messy

What is largely misunderstood by those who don't get to see death on a regular basis is quite how messy it often is. I think the art of undertaking is just that. Those guys can make pretty disfigured and grimacing cadavers look like they are sleeping peacefully. A carefully placed hat or wig may disguise an axe wound to the head, or a bag of straw may provide the illusion of structure in place of the now eviscerated torso. The undertaker is not a magician, though, and I can well imagine that the final product of some of my client's villainy would necessitate a thorough nailing shut of the coffin lid.

What came as a surprise as a newbie to the law was the frequency with which you would be exposed to extremely graphic and horrifying images. It is probably a sad indictment of the trade that, whilst initially shocking, desensitisation followed over time. Lawyers tend to have a morbid sense of humour as I suspect medics, front-line emergency workers and military personnel do too. It helps us deal with the daily unpleasantness to which we are exposed.

## Don't Pick Your Nose

One of the solicitors entered my office to request that I do some work on her case. It was my first exposure to graphic images of death.

Police had made a drugs raid at a second-storey flat in East London after intelligence had led them to suspect that there was a gang of drug dealers peddling crack cocaine and heroin from the property. Two junior police officers remained outside while others bashed down the door and ran inside. The role of the junior police officers was to film the outside of the property so that in the event drugs were disposed of out of the window, there would be a recording which could be used as evidence. I located the disc of the footage within the file and played it on my computer.

The police were seen to enter the property, immediately following which a window opened revealing Mr S, apparently disinclined to engage in acquaintances with the authorities, attempting to escape. Only after exiting the window do I suppose that he appreciated quite how high up he was, clutching onto a drain pipe for as long as he could. Had the park railings below – blunt, 3/4-inch in diameter and painted green – been half an inch further apart he may have lived to tell the tale.

Mr S lost his grip on the drainpipe and he fell two storeys before his left nostril connected with the railing, emitting a horrifying sound. One police officer began to vomit violently at what he had just seen and both officers, who were still very new to service, had to take time away from their job to deal with the emotional impact the event had on them.

None of the horror seemed to deter the other suspects in the house from putting cunning before compassion, however. When the police demanded to know who the drug paraphernalia – kilogram weights, scales, adulterants and self-sealing bags belonged to – they all pointed out of the window towards the deceased!

They don't prepare you for this stuff at law school, nor anywhere else, frankly. I felt a very deep feeling of sadness, as anyone would. James, from the other side of the room, made a quip about the habit of picking one's nose before lobbing over a cuddly duck toy that took pride of place on his desk, bouncing it off the back of my head. Reflection time over, I took that as the signal to shut up and get on with my work.

## If I Had Murdered Her Rather Than Married Her I Would be Out by Now

The fervent opposition to the continued life of one's nearest and dearest is an all too frequent event, and a staple of the criminal lawyer. I can well understand the stresses and strains inherent in relationships from my own disastrous personal life, although I am pleased to reassure the reader that death as a consequence has, at least to date, been avoided.

Often motivated by jealousy or resentment, partners are sometimes motivated to kill.

Mr A had suspected his wife of infidelity. His suspicion may well have had some foundation in reality, given references to 'bum fun' and 'blowjobs' alongside acknowledgements such as 'yes please to all of the above' within text messages exchanged between his late wife and former best friend. These could hardly be interpreted innocently when happened upon by the defendant. Mr A resolved to kill his wife and chose to run her over with his Range Rover, which he accomplished successfully.

I flicked through the crime-scene photos and those of the post mortem. The horror can barely be articulated in words, and I feel it best if I don't try.

Mr A was convicted and given life. Back then, still a relative newbie, I wouldn't have been human had I not been profoundly upset by the images I saw or reflected on the gruesome nature of what can flow from a desire to kill.

## Death by Dangerous Driving

Ms B had been on her bicycle. The articulated lorry to her immediate right took a left turn, dragging her beneath its wheels and swiftly terminating her life. CCTV footage of the event taken from the corner shop nearby showed the moment of decapitation. I was eternally grateful that the footage had no audio.

I suspect that sometimes, even when it is relatively clear that there should be no criminal liability for a catastrophic event, the resulting tremendous loss prompts the commencement of a prosecution as a response to public pressure for some redress. There really was no case against the lorry driver. One can barely imagine the suffering of the deceased`s family but the lorry driver suffered terribly too, having to relive, what was in truth, just a gruesome accident. He was found not guilty by a jury, quite right too. There were no winners here. My thoughts were with the family of the deceased and the innocent accused.

## East London Cannibal

The police had entered Mr C's flat. He was immediately arrested and the scene which had confronted the police on their arrival was photographed. Those photographs were compiled into a bundle and that bundle sat in my hand as I reclined in my chair in the office.

In the kitchen, next to the cereal, were discreet bundles of arms, legs and torsos. In a pan, blanching on the stove, was a piece of cranium complete with tuft of hair, apparently in preparation for consumption.

I forget what work I had been tasked to do on the case but the facts were certainly something I wasn't going to forget in a while. On the face of it, Mr C was affable and approachable, that was until he killed, butchered and ate you. He was as dangerous a psychopath as there could be.

Legally, in circumstances where it is deemed that at the time of the event the defendant is labouring under the symptoms of a mental illness, he can be regarded as 'insane', in line with an archaic legal definition. On a finding of 'insanity' by a jury, premised upon the opinion of psychiatrists, the accused is taken out of the criminal justice system and instead committed to a psychiatric hospital for an indefinite period. This is what happened to Mr C. None of that hullabaloo seemed to quell his appetite, though. Immediately on his reception into Broadmoor high-security psychiatric hospital he killed and attempted to eat a fellow patient.

## Hog Roast

It was a shame for Mr T that the arranged marriage to his beautiful wife had not been going so well. An intuitive detective inspector hypothesised that, given that it was suspected that Mr T liked men on a romantic level, a fulfilling relationship for him with a woman was unlikely. The current hiatus in Mr T's marriage as a result of his wife's disappearance may have been serving him well. Having given in to family pressure to marry, Mr T, the detective theorised, may have rid himself of the freshfaced persona non grata, by doing her in.

The first fly in the ointment in proving this theory was that there was no proof that she was even deceased. The detective inspector obtained a search warrant and sent some young officers down to search the matrimonial home. They returned to the station following a thorough search having found no evidence of anything untoward. Unsatisfied by this, the detective inspector sent them back two days later to search again.

In the intervening period, the neighbours had phoned the police complaining about the antisocial behaviour of Mr T, persisting with a hog roast in the garden for two days. They had grown weary of the smell of grilling pork.

Exploration of the garden revealed a garden incinerator, a galvanised steel dustbin complete with short chimney protruding from the lid, commonly used to burn garden litter. Wisps of smoke still rose from the pipe as PC Smith removed the lid, coming face to face with the skull of Mr T's late wife.

The viewing of terrible things remains a necessary and inevitable part of the job. Over years of viewing images, not just of violence and its consequences, but of all kinds of abuse too, one becomes somewhat numb to it. You will often hear barristers in robing rooms discussing their briefs for the day in a manner of apparent complete indifference, 'a bit of death' they will say, or 'some noncing'. It is almost run-of-the-mill stuff and but a footnote in the professional remit. The apparent insensitivity is not rooted in disrespect or insensitivity; we lawyers focus more on *whether* something happened rather than *what* happened, and there is little time to dwell on matters secondary to the primary focus. The frequency of cases and endless flow of pressure from the many aspects of the job makes us that way, moreover, we have it instilled in us from the embryonic stages of our training that emotions are an impediment to the proper administration of evidence-based justice. Juries are directed to the same view.

That is not to say that all cases do not create real feelings of sadness, whether or not death has resulted. The bad stuff gets compartmentalised in a head space somewhere, a dark place that is best not visited too often.

# Duck

For some unexplained reason, a bloke they called the 'book man' used to visit the office once a week and leave an array of books and toys for sale. He would return some days later, either to collect money from the sales of anything, or otherwise retrieve his stock. I assume he visited offices all over the place. The 'book man' was the source of the bright orange fluffy duck puppet we named 'Ronald' that took up residence either on James's desk, or the hat stand in our room. Inserting your hand in Ronald's bottom, an activity we indulged in frequently, would result in the thing making a very unducklike 'squeak'.

Making the most of the peace resulting from James having a day out of the office, over the low hum of the desk fan and traffic noise coming in through the open window, I was suddenly interrupted by a shouted 'Oi, twat!'.

I swivelled round on my chair, popped my head through the window, and saw James below on the street. He was off to the police station, but had forgotten his mobile phone. Could I retrieve it?

Rather than descend the stairs to meet him on the street – an option I had considered but rejected on the grounds that I couldn't be arsed – we settled on a scheme to pack the phone into the protective cover of the duck's arse, and then drop it from the window into his arms below.

Although the first part of the plan went all right, the return of Ronald back through the window was decidedly less successful. By the time of James's third attempt, quite a crowd had gathered on the street to watch, it not being every day that you see two of the local lawyers hurling puppets about in public. Disappointingly, the attention had also been drawn of Mr 'Make Yourself Indispensable', the senior partner who, unbeknown to James and me, having seen flashes of orange plumage rocketing passed his window two offices below, had entered my room to investigate. He encountered my arse, the rest of my body hanging out of the window as I attempted to catch the cursed duck. His unmistakable dulcet tones as he enunciated the words, 'What the fuck do you think you are doing?' startled me somewhat, stiffening my limbs and causing me to hit the back of my head hard on the window latch. Quickly placing my feet back on terra firma, I turned to face the boss, praying as I did so that James would also realise the grave seriousness of my predicament.

As you know, I had for some time been nurturing an ability to bullshit my way out of tight spots, but I was undeniably challenged to answer the senior partner's question in any meaningful way. Both lost for words, the boss and I took instead to eyeing each other in the midst of an extraordinarily uncomfortable silence that seemed to last forever. He was visibly pissed off and I would have fallen upon the mercy of a break in the frost had it not come through James striking the window not two inches behind me twice more with the duck. On each impact, the thing squeaked as its face squashed against the glass, hesitated for a moment and then dropped back to the street below.

The passing of another thirty seconds or so without activity hinted at a small blessing that, for James, the penny had finally dropped.

'Let me explain,' I said to the boss, but before the next syllable could be uttered, and with admirable velocity, the duck soared in through the open window, hitting my carved wooden pencil holder and sending my pens and highlighters to the four corners of the room. The shouted word, 'Cunt!' could be heard from outside half a second later.

Observing the boss's ashen face appearing at the window, James dived for cover under the awning of the neighbouring fruit and veg shop. The window was shut with a bang and I was addressed, 'If you have time to fuck around, then you are surplus to requirements. Pack your stuff.' And that was it. The boss walked out.

Being a man of eternal optimism, I resolved to pack my cardboard box slowly in the hope that some rapprochement may, with time, present itself. Sure enough, time being the great healer, there was a change of heart, but the occasion had to be marked. The boss dumped a stack of civil files on my floor accompanied by a list of insurmountable tasks calculated to ruin my life for the next four months.

The only silver lining, if any could be found, was the delight that I took in introducing James to his own stack of civil files placed neatly by the boss's secretary on the corner of his desk, where the late Ronald had once sat.

# Police Station Black Market

James and I were generally the best of mates. Scintillating conversations would alternate between work topics and intellectual/philosophical discussions such as 'anal beards, friend or foe?' Indeed, James had even gifted me my ancient wooden pencil holder, hand-carved by naked virgins in Honolulu. I was grateful to him even despite the shock discovery that the same naked virgins had apparently supplied a box-load to the discount household goods shop at the end of the road where they retailed at fifty pence a pop.

It wasn't always the case that we saw eye to eye though, particularly when it came to options for bunking off work. Police stations, whilst enormously busy and occasionally stressful, were sometimes a good way to skive. A police station in the afternoon, for example, might complete by 3pm thereby allowing an early getaway home rather than a return to the office where you would otherwise be inundated with phone calls and requests to work on files. Such skives could be the source of friction, not least because those left in the office would be required to take up the slack.

Among the trainees and pre-trainees who were trying to survive on a pittance, there was something of an underground trade in police station slots and rotas. For overtime purposes they could mean the difference between survival and a financial apocalypse.

As a general rule, I would rather be on the breadline than in Peckham nick at 2am, so I was always willing to give my rota slots away. That said, if there was a police station in the daytime that would mean an escape from the demanding drudgery of the office, then I was prepared to fight dirty for it, and I don't just mean metaphorically either. Not a week after the 'duck incident' one such 'opportunity' sparked an intense fist-fight between James and me in our room. I'll give it to him, he was quite tough, but seemingly ill-prepared for the keenness of my bite and my aptitude with a golf umbrella. The bulk of the brawl was not witnessed by anyone in authority – mercifully – and there were no hard feelings over it. Mr 'Make Yourself Indispensable', however, did observe my final word on the matter which was to launch my stapler across the room, missing its target by a good margin and instead hitting the top of James's monitor with a loud bang. This, as you can probably by now appreciate, did little to help dispel my growing reputation for idiocy. As ever, the punishment was the gift of yet more civil files.

# Journey to the Cop Shop

When somebody has been arrested and due to be interviewed by the police, the course of events for the solicitor generally follows the same pattern. The solicitor is invited into the custody area, provides his details to the custody sergeant and then sits with the investigating officer to receive 'disclosure'.

Disclosure is in essence a Q & A session with the officer concerning the nature of the allegation and the evidence they have. This is when the game begins. By law, the police do not have to disclose anything at all to the lawyer at that stage, and whilst they would love to ambush the accused during their interview with evidence, the courts can take a dim view of such tactics. Case law now dictates that solicitors be able to give informed advice to their clients, which can only be done if they are informed themselves.

Throughout the entire process, from police station through to trial, a defence lawyer's mandate is simple: to act in his or her client's best interests. Within the framework of the law, the advice given is geared either to getting the client off the hook at as early a stage as possible or, alternatively, securing the most lenient sentence if complete exoneration is not feasible. This is the way of the adversarial process. The defence drive is counterbalanced by the opposing prosecutorial one, and justice lies somewhere in between, or that's the theory at any rate.

At the most basic level, there are three options open to a solicitor and his or her client with respect to a police interview:

Option One: No comment.

A fundamental plank of our criminal-justice system is the 'privilege against self-incrimination'. The prosecution bring the case; the defendant doesn't need to prove anything. The accused is accordingly afforded the right to say nothing at any stage of the case, including to the police.

I have, on hundreds of occasions, advised a client to say 'no comment', and for a variety of reasons. Not admitting guilt may be one, but there are also a great many reasons consistent with innocence to take that approach. One example may be that the police have insufficient evidence, are unlikely to get any more, and so, notwithstanding how innocent or guilty the client may be, or professes to be, it may be remiss of a lawyer to advise comment, thereby exposing the client to potential evidence-gathering through interrogation.

For another example, imagine a scenario where a client instructs his brief that he couldn't have been thieving from Tesco, because he was at home murdering his flatmate at the time. It is probably in the client's interests not to give the

...

police that account, despite it providing a rock-solid alibi for the accusation of shoplifting. I am sure you get the point.

Alternatively, the accused may be insufficiently articulate or in some other way unable to do him or herself justice in the interview, whether through youth, illness or some other limitation.

These are just a few illustrations of an almost endless list of occasions when a 'no comment' interview does not necessarily imply the guilt of the accused.

There are potential consequences to a 'no comment' interview, though, that require serious consideration. The main one is that a court or jury can be invited to hold that fact against the defendant in certain prescribed circumstances, most notably when it is considered to have been 'reasonable' to expect an answer in interview similar to the one he or she advances in court. The defendant would have been cautioned about this at the beginning of the interview: 'You do not have to say anything, but it may harm your defence if you do not mention when questioned something you later rely on in court, anything you do say may be used in evidence.' That is what it means. When is it reasonable not to answer questions? That is up to the jury, with a little help from the lawyers of course!

Regardless of the complexity of the associated legal directions on this topic, doubtless the jury will have watched crime dramas and seen the demonstrably guilty saying, 'No comment'. The lawyer must be attuned to these practical realities and poised to correct prejudices.

Option Two: Answer questions.

If the police already have sufficient evidence for a case, and the client has a defence, the usual starting point is advise them to answer the questions. A convincing account of events could be given, further investigation undertaken, and a charge might even be avoided, along with the adverse consequences described above. The downside of this option is the abundant potential for the client to make a complete pig's balls of it, either leading the police to more evidence or exposing themself as a liar. Neither of these options would lend to a restful night's sleep for the client or their brief.

Option Three: Half-way house – the submission of a 'prepared statement'.

Rather than answer the questions orally, the client can instead submit a pre-prepared statement to the police during the course of the interview and is thereby deemed to have answered questions. In some circumstances this can be a neat way of avoiding the possibility of adverse inferences being drawn from a 'no comment' response to questions. A written statement allows for precision and control. To use the example above, a statement could succinctly identify the alibi for the Tesco theft but omit the admission that there was a concurrent murder of a flatmate.

The downside of this option is the possibility that insufficient detail may be given to entirely avoid the adverse consequences of a complete 'no comment' interview should the client expand on his account later during trial. Additionally, a jury is bound to speculate as to why, if the accused could advance an account in the form of a statement, they couldn't simply have spoken to the police and subjected the account to the process of interrogation. Again, the lawyer must be attuned to these considerations and ready to deal with the possible consequences of choices made.

I have summarised in a paragraph or two the types of considerations that confront a police station brief, but this is a topic about which books the size of a small motorhome have been written. To settle on the right advice requires the forecasting of various future scenarios, including the way the topics may ultimately be articulated before a judge and by a defence barrister to a jury. There are so many considerations to juggle, and in the face of almost certainly inadequate information from the police, and sometimes even less from the client. At no other time in criminal proceedings is one faced with so much uncertainty. The only limiting factor to one's mastery as a police station representative is brain power. The work is tactical and demands a stratagem.

The police interview sets the course and foundation for the whole case and can literally make or break it. To give you a picture; imagine, in a complete lack of sleep, multiple detainees requiring your services, pressure and isolation in a hostile environment. For want of funds for a taxi ride home afterwards, let's not forget the exigency of looking over your shoulder as you walk back up Walworth High Street from the nick at 3am, lest you be stabbed. Now you have an idea of the experience of the police station brief.

## Fucking Piggy Wiggies!

Young Master J was endlessly in trouble, always getting arrested for some indiscretion or other, and had amassed what is euphemistically described in the trade as, an 'unenviable' record of previous convictions. His recidivism, and loyalty to the firm, made him a 'good client'; one to keep happy, and I was off to the police station to represent him.

He wasn't formally a client of our team, he was 'Make Yourself Indispensable's', not that he had ever had anything to do with him in his life; his trainees invariably represented J and did all the necessary case preparation in those of his cases that proceeded to court. I considered it judicious, therefore, to pop next door and get the lowdown from the trainee, Sam, who knew him well. 'I have never advised J to answer questions,' he said. 'Leaving aside for a moment the fact that he is a complete arsehole, he never tells the truth and messes it up.'

On this particular occasion, J had been arrested on suspicion of burgling a cannabis factory. Cannabis factories are often set up in ordinary houses, converted for the purpose. Windows are blacked out, electricity by-passed, and powerful lights and fans installed to promote the crop. A converted two-up, two-down terraced house could potentially yield up to one million pounds street value of cannabis per annum. Some relatively hardened, seasoned, not to mention violent, criminals get involved in these enterprises. It goes without saying, then, that being a nine-stone street urchin, as Master J was, and having burgled one, tends to put you at the front of the queue for a diet of hospital food. The fact that, Vietnamese 'farmers' possessed of sharp gardening tools wished to have a 'chat' with J came second to the fact that, right now, so did the police, and did little to assuage the 'fizziness' that was a notable quality of Mr J's personality.

I received disclosure from the officer, being apprised of the overwhelming case that they had against him, before being ushered into a small room in the custody area for my private consultation with J.

He was seventeen years old, blond-haired, thin, with sunken cheek bones and reeking of cannabis; pretty much your standard. He asked me what they said he had done. I told him and it was only at this juncture that things became a trifle unconventional. Standing on his chair and pulling himself up tall, he began to chant, 'Piggy wiggies, fucking piggy wiggies, bastard fucking piggy wiggies!' while simultaneously leaping up and down, with the occasional interruption resulting from his striking his head forcefully against the wall.

Not to be deterred, I invested five minutes or so in a calming operation and J became sufficiently lucid to give me an account of events. In fairness, it was a not completely ridiculous one, relatively speaking. He had a defence, and I could see no impediment to his answering questions in the police interview. I simply couldn't understand why the other lawyers at the firm had always advised J to give a 'no comment' interview, regardless of the circumstances. 'Answer questions!', was my advice.

Two police officers, the client and I gathered in a police interview room. The tapes were started, the caution was given and the first question asked. I fully expected J to deny the accusation, but instead he replied: 'When this interview ends I am going to fucking knock you out!'

As the colour drained from my face and a little panic set in, the cautionary words of Sam the trainee started to creep up from the pit of my stomach. Had the whole 'Fucking Piggy Wiggies' display and the head-shaped dents in the wall been a terrible omen of things to come?

The second question didn't elicit any improvement, neither did a firm kick under the table. In fact, J professed with ever-increasing enthusiasm that when the interview concluded he was going to 'fucking knock them out!' In fact, he made the same claim in response to every single question that was put to him over the next thirty, hellish minutes.

At the end of the interview, J remained in custody and I left the police station feeling considerably deflated, but better informed of J's idiosyncrasies. I resolved never to advise that he answer questions again. It was at about 3am that a call came to the bleep phone notifying me of a new case at the police station, this time concerning an assault. J had beaten up three police officers, knocking one unconscious.

I phoned Sam the next morning. 'How did it go?' he enquired.

'You were wrong about J,' I replied. 'He tells the truth.'

## Strike Like a Snake

Generally speaking, the police and defence briefs got along just fine. At the very least there is cordiality, and sometimes even a friendly rapport. We were adversaries, though, and there was no escaping the fact that, in their eyes, you were the bad guys: interrupting the administration of justice rather than being an essential part of it. An opportunity to make a brief's life uncomfortable was not one that your average police officer would pass up. For this reason, it was James's policy never to accept an offer of a cup of tea when at the nick; this was my policy too.

Cynically, the local nick had removed the inside door handle from the consultation room in the custody area. The rationale, they claimed, was to ensure that the detainee would remain detained when speaking with his brief, and prevented from making a menace of himself around the main atrium of the custody suite. What did not seem to concern the police one jot was the fact that the person who was disposed to creating mischief in the custody area would instead be trapped in a small room with the brief; or rather, the brief would be trapped with him. On the contrary, I suspect that this was all part of the plan.

Mr R was a heroin addict who was in a profound state of drug withdrawal at the time I met him. He had been arrested on suspicion of viciously attacking his girlfriend, which included pulling out handfuls of her hair as he dragged her from room to room around their flat. He had sprayed lighter fluid all round the place as his young kids slept upstairs and with a lighter in hand had threatened to burn everyone to death unless his girlfriend overcame her embarrassment and asked for money from the neighbours to purchase more heroin.

He told me that he was entirely innocent, and that the whole thing was a grotesque fabrication unless, of course, I could get him some sort of plea deal later in proceedings or, more importantly, some bail before court. That being the case, he might be prepared to reconsider the question of whether he was, in fact, guilty or not! The proud owner of over one hundred prior convictions for drugs, theft and violence, he was definitely the sort of person that would motivate you to cross over the road when spotted at one hundred yards.

Generally speaking, I would say that the majority of clients one meets are compliant, sometimes even polite and appreciative of your work, regardless of their history or personal circumstances. Some can be a little more fractious, especially if withdrawing from heroin, but dealing with irascible drug users is just part of the daily grind. Occasionally clients have little to redeem them, some are even pretty horrible. And then, once in a while one meets a client like R, the sort of person that, were it not for the C word being available for reference to him, the world would be a much poorer place. You get the picture.

The police had already made it clear that he was going to be charged with offences and remanded in custody to attend court the next day; there was no chance of bail.

Not that any of this should have been a surprise to him; he hadn't left via the front door of a police station for years. Quiet resignation to the fact was what I expected; quiet resignation was not what resulted.

When I was a kid, a best mate of mine once tricked me into attempting to capture a stray goose with the aid of a golf umbrella. The news of Mr R's impending incarceration was similarly well received. It was with great enthusiasm that he made his displeasure known. He was impulsive, dangerous, on his feet and in my face, all of which added a certain *je ne sais quoi* to his insistent observation that I was 'a useless cunt'.

My tried-and-tested tactic to diffuse such situations, was to play the bespectacled and swotty mummy's boy, pleading mercy in the face of humbling machismo. As much smoke as I could feasibly blow up this maniac's arse was accordingly blown. There were also promises of immediate restoration of liberty, spoken soothingly in a tone of motherly nurture. Ordinarily, I wouldn't have bothered trying to neutralise such hostilities. Instead, I would have run out into the custody area to summon the assistance of a load of coppers. And this would have been my remedy of choice here had it not been for the sadistic bastard who had removed the door handle.

At the same time as I was pleading for mercy, I was quietly hitting the panic button in the room. In fact I hit it repeatedly, about thirty times with increasing desperation. The button sets off a loud alert that can be heard by the entire area – which at this time was occupied by about twenty police officers – and probably the whole neighbourhood beyond. Did anybody come to my aid? Did they chuff.

Playing the surrender monkey suited me as a first line of defence, but that was not to say that I didn't also have a firm grasp of the chair in full preparedness to break it across my client's teeth and render him decisively incapacitated, should the need arise. I hadn't spent my youth pitching myself against my amateur boxer brother to mature into a big pair of frilly knickers in adulthood; I could strike like a snake and bite like a crocodile if provoked. With the planned element of surprise promising effectiveness of my defence, I hadn't altogether dismissed my chances, and the disaccord between my client and me could very well have resulted in a bloodbath had it not been for the fact that – a full five minutes after I had first pushed the panic button and after enough time for me to be very dead – a police officer opened the door.

As I dropped the chair and wiped the sweat from my brow, he asked nonchalantly 'Did you call, sir?'

## The Poopster

By the time I had encountered this client at the police station I had been doing the job for some time and was relatively seasoned. I was well attuned to handling the police, their jolly japes and wizard wheezes, and to smelling when something was a little 'off'.

The officer in charge of the investigation refused to bring my client out of his cell. He told me that he had been 'disruptive' and would I mind speaking to him privately through the wicket of the cell.

A cell wicket is a small, sliding hatch in the cell door, large enough to pass food and communicate with a detainee, but too small for him to climb through. As a rule, a solicitor is entitled to see their client for a conference in a setting conducive to the task, although I had, on occasion, sat with a client in a cell when other facilities were unavailable. I wasn't particularly happy at the officer's suggestion, but introductions through a wicket were no great imposition; the days when I would have a tear-up with the police over a point of principle were long gone, unless the point was vital to the case. I learned from experience that such conflicts tended to result only in a lengthy wait outside in the reception area. I chose my battles carefully. Diplomacy and stealth translated to better results all round.

I was led to the back of the custody area to the row of cells just as a cleaner walked out of the corridor with his mop and bucket, making way for the officer and me. Cell number four was the only one with its wicket shut.

'You know how to open the wicket don't you?' said the officer.

He ushered me towards the cell. This was very unusual indeed. A police officer would, at the very least, be expected to open the wicket and introduce the brief. Smelling a large rat, I refused and instead invited the officer to do the honours. By this time, I had already asked myself what a large boat hook was doing in a police station. I was about to find out.

With both hands on the boat hook, and at a distance of two metres or so, the officer skilfully released the latch on the wicket. The look of expectation on his face for a moment or two was soon explained when a large clod of excrement rocketed through the open wicket and exploded on the whitewashed wall behind. Further discharges of poo were fired out in rapid succession, peppering the wall and floor as I took cover behind a pedal bin. The officer turned on a sixpence with his back to the wall, signalled for back-up like a general who had just unturfed the enemy.

The rationale underpinning my client's 'dirty protest' remains one of life's imponderables, albeit throwing shit at police officers is not always remarkable, nor indeed unwarranted. I couldn't help but have some respect for the officer's ruse to put me in the firing line. If I'm honest with myself, and had the boot been on the other foot, I would surely have done the same. I gave the officer a look of congratulatory acknowledgement, the sort that only blokes give to one another when a successful, or near-successful, stitch-up of their mate has occurred, and left to deal with another client, while awaiting the completion of yet another clean-up mission. The officer, with equal skill, negotiated the wicket shut before once again summoning the poor cleaner who had already spent the afternoon clearing up similar such offerings from my client's arse.

It wasn't until some hours later, complete with paper onesie, mercifully empty bowels and a promise of good behaviour, that my client was shown to the interview room for his consultation with me.

For a man with a propensity for excrement sharing, merely peeing his pants when in conference with me was of minimal concern; there were more than enough dry chairs for everyone to sit on. I popped out to inform the police what had happened and to get the place cleaned up, but had barely advanced from the threshold when some sort of divine inspiration held me back, call it a good idea if you will. Turning back to face my client, I asked him to allow me to provide him with a dry seat.

Purely in pursuit of my client's comfort, I swapped the interviewer's chair with his, staying well clear of the urine-saturated foam as I did so. Imagining, as I did, that the soiled chair would soon be occupied by the attentive police officer who, not long before, had sought to place me in the line of a faecal fusillade. I was greatly pained by the anticipation of his displeasure. I regretted even more the actual discomfort suffered by the officer as I witnessed him shuffling and rocking from one leg to another throughout the interview, unable to express any objection as the interview tapes rolled uninterrupted for forty-five minutes.

When all is said and done, my own moral discomfort at this unpleasantness had to give way to the rules of professional practice: to act in my client's best interests. Shafting the police officer was simply collateral to that.

It hurt me, but what else could I have done?

## Your Great Auntie Fanny

Contrary to popular belief, defence lawyers do not provide their clients with a defence, or at least they shouldn't. Not only would that be a grave breach of our professional rules, it would also amount to perverting the course of justice. Having said that, defence lawyers are entitled, or indeed obliged, to advise their clients of the law governing the alleged offence and the legal defences available. To that end, hypothetical examples might be used in order to articulate the concepts. If the client has half a brain and is somewhat unscrupulous, which, let's face it, he will be, he will wait to hear from his lawyer as to the state of evidence and legal defences available, before imparting his account of events.

It would be unsurprising, then, if that account aligned neatly with one of the recognised defences explained to him moments before. A conversation might go thus: 'You have been identified as headbutting Tyler Smith in Snobs nightclub. The evidence that it was you is overwhelming. There are a number of defences to a charge of assault, the primary ones being: having an alibi; acting in self-defence; and acting in defence of another. You are entitled to act reasonably, even pre-emptively, in defence of yourself. The key word here is 'reasonably'. The level of reactive force justified will be considered with reference to the opposing threat. For example, if you are punched and you punch back, motivated only by your self-preservation, then your response may be regarded as reasonable. If you then went on to stab your attacker once the threat from him had diminished, that would be a clear example of having gone beyond that which is reasonable. If you are confronted with potentially fatal violence, on the other hand, you might be justified in using a greater intensity of force. Do you understand? So what happened, pal?'

'Er, I was acting in self-defence, guv.'

'Right, well how do you justify the Glasgow kiss?'

'He had a broken bottle in his hand.'

'Well done, you have been paying attention in class.'

Mr T, the gentleman whose interests I had come to represent on this particular day, had been arrested on suspicion of assaulting his partner; this had been witnessed not only by the alleged victim herself, but also by a number of neighbours. I had been struggling for some time to explain the salient principles to Mr T. He did not appear to be the sharpest tool in the box, but I had nevertheless had my best stab at explaining the main defences against a charge of assault, including self-defence.

I gave him the lowdown: 'You have been seen by a number of people who know you, and have no reason to lie, repeatedly hitting your partner with a table leg. There is strong evidence of identification. One of the primary defences against a charge of assault is self-defence. Another defence,' I said, 'is alibi. Do you know what I mean when I say alibi?'

'No.'

'It means you weren't there, which in this case would mean that all of the witnesses that say otherwise are either lying, or mistaken.' I raised my eyebrows. 'Do you follow?'

Mr T looked at me blankly, so I continued,

'If you weren't at home assaulting your partner at all, but instead at your great Auntie Fanny's house, for example, then you would have a defence of alibi. Do you understand?' I continued. 'That would mean, of course, that you would be asking the police, and probably a court, to consider that all of these witnesses who say you were there, are lying. They would be unlikely to buy it.'

I thought I saw a glimmer of light in his eyes, but it was probably just a reflection from the strip bulb.

'Just forget it, I digress. Let me explain the defence of self-defence a bit more…'

I wasn't really sure what he was going to say in the interview other than, 'I didn't do it,' but, satisfied that he must at the very least have realised that any suggestion of alibi was a non-starter, and having found the end of my tether, I called the cops in to make a start.

After switching on the tapes and alluding to the accounts of a million-and-one witnesses who saw Mr T at the crime scene, the police officer asked Mr T for his account of events.

'I wasn't at home assaulting my partner,' said Mr T earnestly, 'I was at my Great Auntie Fanny's house'.

'Could we have a short break in the interview for a private consultation with my client?' I asked the officer serenely.

'Already?' The officer looked at me askance. 'We have only just begun!'

'Yes, please.'

The police officers filed out of the room and there followed a heavy thud as my head hit the table. I assume that the words I then uttered were muffled owing to my face being pressed against the table-top in despair.

'What did you say, sir?'

I lifted my head and looked my client in the eyes before speaking slowly and clearly,

'You don't have a fucking Great Auntie Fanny!'

## Local Lad

It seemed that the guy I was due to represent down at the local nick on this particular morning harboured some prejudice towards me for being the 'strong in the arm, thick in the head' country-dwelling-cretin type, that I am the first to admit, I am. He wanted a cockney as his brief, full stop. I couldn't be arsed to argue my impressive credentials to this moron; besides, my colleague Rob was coming down to take over which freed me up for a crafty bunk. It wasn't long before the silhouette of the broad-shouldered and bald-headed Rob came into view as he swaggered confidently towards the police station. All misty-eyed and with apparent vindication, my client pointed over to him and proudly announced, 'There you are, son! That is what I call a local, London lad!'

'Whey aye, man, what ye up tee?' came Rob, in his almost indecipherable Geordie accent.

## Run for the Hills

I saw Mr HM at Stratford shopping mall as I made my way back to the office from the local nick. Mr HM was a former client of Suzie, one of the solicitors in the firm. I didn't recall what Mr HM had been charged with on that particular occasion, or what work I had done on the case, but I did remember that Mr HM was as mad as a bag of badgers. His insanity paired nicely with his piercing eyes and shock of chaotic, curly hair. It was a very bad error of judgement for me to say, 'Hi H!'

On seeing me, HM began to make Gorilla noises at the same time as waving his arms in the air as if dancing to 'Agadoo' on a cheap package holiday. To my surprise, and that of a number of carefree elderly shoppers whose newspapers and shopping bags were disturbed as I darted by, a keen pursuit quickly followed. I fancy myself as a relatively decent cross-country runner, but HM had an unnerving turn of speed. I lost him, eventually, but not before I was at least half a mile away from my starting point.

## Detention Clock Unconsciousness

Ms O'R was an approachable, middle-aged woman arrested on suspicion of various distraction burglaries, credit-card frauds and other deception offences; she was clearly adept at duping people.

Ordinarily an arrestee can only be detained for twenty-four hours unless, before the expiration of that time, an extension is granted. This can be for up to thirty-six hours or, exceptionally, up to seventy-two hours for particularly serious and complex investigations. If the twenty-four hours expire before a charge is brought or an extension granted, then the police must, by law, release the suspect. If they refuse, they are guilty of wrongfully imprisoning someone. That's the theory at least, as explained by the lecturers at my university and as described here in my 'Noddy's Guide to Police Station Representation' book.

It was following Ms O'R's interview that I sat with her next to the custody desk awaiting a charging decision. There was quite a queue in front of us and I noticed that there were only five minutes left on the detention clock. I said to Ms O'R, 'There are five minutes left on the detention clock. When you are charged you will undoubtedly be remanded in custody to appear in court the next day given your "unenviable" record of previous convictions. If they haven't charged you within five minutes, on the other hand, they will have no choice but to release you. Let's lie low and see if the time won't pass away.'

I was definitely not intimating that my client should feign unconsciousness with a view to timing out the detention clock. Nevertheless, with an over-exaggerated sigh, Ms O'R slumped to the floor, lying spreadeagled and motionless in a truly Oscar-winning performance that even had me concerned for all of about half a second.

A far cry from my suggestion that we just keep a low profile, the resulting pandemonium was phenomenal; police officers swarmed in from miles around in general panic.

When in plain view of police onlookers, and with an expression of sincere concern on my face, I crouched down and said comfortingly to the casualty, 'Ms O'R, are you all right?!'

Out of sight of spectators, I kicked her hard in the arse and spat out the words, 'What the fucking hell do you think you're doing?'

A sly eye opened occasionally for the invalid to glance quickly at the clock before returning to its 'resting peacefully in an untimely passing' state. Miraculously, as soon as six minutes had elapsed, there was an apparent complete revival.

It may have been a bit flippant of me to exclaim that we had all just witnessed a miracle, neither did it do much to prepare the custody sergeant for my next comment: 'By the way, the detention clock has expired and you are now duty-bound to release my client forthwith, lest you be held responsible for unlawfully detaining her.'

With that, the sergeant summoned two other officers, 'Get this idiot out of here!' were his words.

Like an underage reveller caught puking in the corner of a bar being expelled by doormen, I was wrestled to the door and bounced out of the nick and onto the street.

'And don't come back!' is what they didn't say whilst slapping the dust from their hands, but were words I half expected.

It seems that the police considered that I must have been complicit in this ludicrous hoax, and took the decision to charge Ms O'R in my absence and remand her in custody for the night.

Maybe I had grounds for complaint, but was I really going to pursue the police for wrongful imprisonment for twenty minutes or so? Or complain about my improper expulsion? Of course I wasn't; such action would be entirely futile and, in any event, there were now unsettling suggestions of unprofessionalism on my part being bandied about, despite my complete innocence.

It was best to let sleeping dogs lie, for want of a better expression, and return my head firmly to its default position: below the parapet.

## You Have Your Solicitor Present and a Dustbin to Puke In

In my early days of representing suspects in police stations I would struggle to sleep on the nights that followed, agonising over whether or not I had given the correct advice. As time went on, I became more confident, competent and phlegmatic. Rumour has it that the best surgeons are those with the least compassion, and I suppose that similar principles apply to lawyers. I was focused on doing the best job I could, but as to the outcome for the client, I became a little more detached over time.

Dr P was the police station Force Medical Examiner, or FME. In other words, he was the doctor who would be called out to deal with suspects who had medical complaints whilst at the police station. He would also certify whether a suspect was medically fit to be interviewed. Dr P would always, without exception to my knowledge, certify a detainee as fit for interview regardless of whether they were fit or not. As a consequence, Dr P, and any investigating officer who acted in line with Dr P's unfortunate assessments, became my staunch adversary.

There have been times when, courtesy of Dr P, I have sat in police interviews with persons so mentally disordered that they had no concept of what was happening to them. On each occasion, after every bizarre comment that would be made in response to a question, I would chime in and say, 'My client is currently suffering from the symptoms of a mental illness and is unfit to be interviewed'. That tended to unnerve the interrogators sufficiently for them to take appropriate action, failing which it helped to set out my stall for later argument in court.

By the time I met Mr R, though, I had already dealt with five different suspects and their police interviews that day. It was getting late, I was knackered, stinking of sweat, and had five new case files to open, police station notes to write up and all the other associated administration to do on top of my office workload. I really wanted to go home.

The allegation was that Mr R had lent himself to a spree of car jackings; in other words, he had been robbing drivers of their cars. It was a serious allegation. The investigating officers had their concerns about Mr R's fitness for interview as he had complained of feeling sick and appeared under the weather. Sensibly, they were proposing to delay the interview until later in the evening, albeit at a time when I would ordinarily be tucked up in bed. The appropriate thing to have done would have been to acquiesce in that suggestion and return later. Instead, I did something so grossly injurious and self-serving that I still regret it to this day. I got him assessed by the doctor.

I take this opportunity to apologise unreservedly to Mr R for him spending his interview vomiting into a dustbin hastily thrown his way by the police officer, to the jury for having to listen to that interview; and I extend my gratitude to my regulatory body for not striking me off. I am not proud.

## Murder

Mr Q had been arrested on suspicion of a notorious and high-profile murder. He was an old client of the senior partner, not 'Make Yourself Indispensable', but his brother in arms, who was equally, if not yet more, obnoxious. This was certainly the sort of thing that a senior solicitor should have attended to and not a trainee, but there was no way he was going to go to the police station for three days. The task fell to me.

The investigating officers were senior members of the murder squad and they made sure you knew it, strutting around the station in American-style bomber jackets with loud gold emblems that announced their identity. They were arrogant, imperious and impossible to deal with.

To receive disclosure prior to the interview, I was made to stand in an unfurnished room with a number of police officers. I had nowhere to rest my pad of paper to take notes and obtaining information from them was like extracting blood from a stone. All of this was designed to add pressure, to make me feel ambushed and throw me off my game, leaving the door open for the police to ambush my client with potentially incriminating evidence as yet unseen by me.

A 'phased disclosure' tactic was adopted – feeding small amounts of information to the lawyer, conducting an interview, drip-feeding a little more, interviewing again, and so on. The idea is to not give too much away and tease answers out of the suspect that later evidence, hitherto undisclosed, could undermine. With extensions granted to the detention clock of up to seventy-two hours, by the end of three days at the police station there had been a total of six interviews.

It transpired that automatic number plate readers, CCTV footage and mobile-phone data all provided evidence of the presence of my client and his car at the murder scene. Moreover, the car had later been observed to stop and deposit an item. This was subsequently recovered and identified as the murder weapon.

Mr Q had a good defence. In essence, he was simply the driver for others who had caused the fatal wound, of which he had initially been ignorant. The trouble was that the people he named as being the culprits were members of a notorious and dangerous criminal gang.

It was late in the evening, about four interviews in, when it appeared necessary to me for Mr Q to consider giving an account of himself. Understandably, he became most exercised at the prospect of giving names, so I phoned the partner to ask his advice.

'Give the names,' he said. 'The account means nothing unless you give the names.'

And that is what I advised, the positive outcome being that, by the end of it all, the defendant had been acquitted by a jury at the Old Bailey. Others were arrested following the defendant's interview and, as a result of what we had done in the police station, were not so fortunate. Despite being a free man, the decision made at the police station to give names put Mr Q's life in danger, and didn't do much good for the safety of mine either.

The partner came to my office a week later. The firm, because of what had happened, had by this time already gained the reputation among the more significant London criminals as being the firm that assisted a 'grass'.

'Why did you name names?' he barked. 'Look what you have done to our reputation.'

Before I had a chance to retort, 'What the fuck?', consider calling him an arsehole or even to bludgeon him right there and then with the hat stand, he had turned on his heels and left. The whole episode was attributed to a rush of blood to the head of an inexperienced, over-enthusiastic trainee.

Bastard.

# Off to the Funny Farm

Before a trainee can qualify as a fully-fledged solicitor, he or she is required to do a stint in various 'seats'. Of course, crime was my primary selection so where I was to spend most of my time. However, I also spent some months in the family department, which I detested, and mental health.

No other trainee before me had chosen the mental-health department for a seat and my decision came as a surprise to the powers that be. There appeared to be no opposition, though, and the lone solicitor who headed up the mental health department was grateful for the help.

The job of the mental health lawyer relates to the law and procedure as it operates to detain in hospital those with a severe mental illness; the majority of a mental health lawyer's time is spent advocating on behalf of those detained with a view to securing their timely release. Of course, a decision to detain a person against their will amounts to a significant incursion into that person's life. The scrutiny within the gift of the lawyer, therefore, is sacrosanct.

I chose the mental-health department for two reasons: the first being that I would continue to meet weird and wonderful people; the second being that I would be required to conduct advocacy at mental-health tribunals and 'hospital managers' meetings', furnishing me with valuable skills. These hearings are constituted to consider the question of continued detention; the former are a little more formal than the latter, but with the same mandate.

Most clients with whom I dealt were either detained under Section 3 of the Mental Health Act or, alternatively, Section 37 which, while largely similar in form and operation, is the section concerning a mental-health disposal from the criminal justice system. The law permits a person to be detained for treatment if: a) the nature of their symptoms is such that their detention is 'appropriate'; and b) that it is necessary for the safety of the patient, or protection of others, that they should receive such treatment; and c) it cannot be provided unless they are detained under the section.

I am sure you can well imagine the sorts of arguments constructed for the purposes of a legal application for discharge. Usually, the most important things for a patient to demonstrate are insight into their illness alongside a resolve to continue with treatment following discharge from hospital. In my experience, I seldom encountered any genuine insight. Most were so away with the fairies that they would never accept the notion that they were unwell. Occasionally, those detained for long enough learned sufficiently to pretend that they had insight into their illness and a resolve to be medicated for the purposes of the hearing. In truth, they had no such thing. One client of mine, for example, professed that when the TV spoke to her commanding her to attack a neighbour in return for prizes, she now recognised that this was but a manifestation of a mental disorder and not the bidding of the Almighty. The second she was allowed some leave from hospital, she made a beeline for the neighbour's house with a can of petrol and a lighter, on the premise that she was in line for a holiday in Bermuda and a new microwave oven.

The psychiatrists would generally see through this. Moreover, they tended not to detain people unless really necessary. For these reasons, securing a discharge at a hearing was notoriously difficult. I failed ninety-nine per cent of the time, but had fun in trying. And, at the very least, I gained valuable experience in arguing persuasively despite having no personal faith in the argument's substance: a valuable skill for an advocate.

### It Wasn't Me

R, a sixteen-year-old boy, was a new client and one of my first in my new seat at the mental health department. He had been detained at the Maudsley Hospital after exhibiting some symptoms of psychosis. Ordinarily, a conference room on the ward would be found for the solicitor/patient meeting, but on this day none was available. The senior psychiatrist kindly offered us his office for a meeting on condition that we didn't touch anything.

The conference had gone well. R seemed comparatively balanced and discerning and I began to wonder why he had been brought into hospital for assessment. It looked like he had a good case. It wasn't until about seven minutes in that, without any apparent provocation or trigger that I could see, he proceeded with great enthusiasm, not to mention wanton aggression, to entirely deconstruct the doctor's office. From my shelter behind a cupboard door, I remember my surprise at just how many pieces a once perfectly serviceable desk phone could be reduced to, now that it lay in pieces all over the room. After thirty seconds, R returned to his lucid state just as rapidly as he had lost it, and we both now sat in a bomb zone where an office had once stood. I was stunned, unable to speak, but R babbled away cordially as if nothing had happened.

It was at this moment that the doctor walked in, doubtless alerted by the sound of smashing glass and the thud-thudding of medical books and files hitting the floor. He appeared speechless for a moment, gazing around his room open-mouthed and aghast, mesmerised at the devastation that confronted him.

Now, seeing as the doctor, an intelligent young man, could see only two people, a smartly-dressed trainee solic-itor and a violent psychopath in for assessment, I found his question a little jarring: 'Who did this?'

Had I been the more contemptuous and long-in-the-tooth lawyer that I am now I would have replied politely, 'Take a wild guess, you fucking buffoon!'

I wasn't, unfortunately, I was still a relatively green trainee, not to mention respectful. Out of some misplaced loyalty to my client, and mindful of my professional duties of confidentiality and to act in my client's best interests, I settled instead on, 'Well, it wasn't me!'

I hoped that through a process of deduction, a well-educated gentleman such as the doctor would be guided to the correct answer.

## Put Your Penis Away, Please

I was off to a tribunal for Mr K at the hospital. As I walked through the lounge area of the ward on my way to see the client, I acknowledged a few of my other clients.

Ms M, a ruddy-faced middle-aged woman accosted me by the doors. She was hoping to be discharged from hospital soon; her hearing was fast approaching. She had a quiet word in my ear having first checked over her shoulder guardedly lest somebody overhear. She remarked as to the expediency of leaving the place via my hair or, alternatively, concealed within my carrier bag, an altogether more likely route to freedom than as a result of a tribunal decision. She was probably right, poor devil.

I gave a little wave to Mr T, now in his seventies, who had been detained in hospital for the past thirty years since killing his wife. He was an old client of my supervising solicitor, a very personable gentleman, sadly never likely to get out. I suspect that the years of confinement and compulsory cocktails of psychotropic medication had not done him a world of good, although they probably had served to prevent any further love interest meeting a sticky end. He wouldn't even be able to cope on his own now.

My client on this day, Mr K, had been doing really well by contrast. His medical notes alluded to greater displays of insight, compliance on the ward, less sexual disinhibition and a marked lessening of his grandiose ideation. He certainly made all the right noises as I prepared him for the forthcoming hearing. I was yet to secure a discharge from hospital for anyone, but I hoped that this would be the one.

The hearing could not have gone better. As far as I was concerned it was certain that there would be a discharge. My only question was whether or not my exquisite cross-examination of the psychiatrist would lead to some tangible acclamation that I could hang on my office wall. All that needed to happen now was for the client to sit quietly during the completion of my 'Rumpole of the Bailey' closing address, and we would all be out in a jiffy.

As is often the case, confidence comes before a fall and, like the shattering of shop windows, it was just at the point that I was barrel-rolling in self-congratulation, that Mr K offered up some dire words that struck me with an icy chill and caused a sharp intake of breath.

'I need to remove my trousers,' he announced.

Hoping that nobody else had heard those terrifying words, I attempted to continue with a trifle more haste and volume, but just before I was able to rest my case, the chairwoman piped up, 'Please don't!' she pleaded.

Behind me, my client's trousers were already around his knees. Even two nurses who had grabbed hold of an arm each as he had begun to remove his outer garments were unsuccessful in preventing the emergence of his penis. Pleas from around the table fell on deaf ears and blushes were only mitigated by the forceful manhandling of Mr K out of the room. The manner of his removal dawned an unfortunate penile helicopter act, which only added insult to already irreparable injury. A chair was knocked over, the door slammed shut with a bang and the hearing was restored to silence, absent Mr K and his pythona non grata.

After a moment or two to gather her thoughts, the chairwoman asked me graciously, 'Do you have any more submissions?'

'No. Thanks.'

### The Non-Believers
I saw Mr S today. He had been detained for some time by reason of some deeply-rooted paranoid ideation and operation of command delusions. Among other peculiar beliefs, he was firmly of the view that his mission in life was to rid the world of all of the 'non-believers'. I had a chat with him and reviewed his medical notes. He was clearly very unwell, obviously dangerous and a hearing with a view to securing his discharge at this time would be entirely futile. I bid my farewell with the promise to monitor the case and keep the position under review.

Despite my having moved to the mental-health department, I was still on the police station rota in the night-time. A week after my last meeting with Mr S, the bleep phone rang. I was required to attend Forest Gate police station. Unimaginably, Mr S's medical team had deemed him well enough to be discharged from hospital. Less unimaginably, he had now been arrested in the bushes of Stratford Park brandishing a large machete.

In my private consultation with Mr S, he instructed me that he had indeed been in the bushes with the knife but, it was okay', he assured me, he was merely on a mission to 'rid the world of the unbelievers'. Crikey!

Emphatically reassuring Mr S that, I myself, was as staunch a believer as anyone he could shake a shitty stick at, I suggested that he decline to answer the police questions. Funnily enough, I didn't feel that a frank confession of murderous intent would improve his personal situation much.

Mr S having followed my advice, left the police in complete ignorance of his true motivations. It was out of real concern for the safety of the general public that I tipped the wink to the police officer in charge to seek a medical assessment of Mr S and to make contact with his psychiatrist before there could be any suggestion of releasing him back into the community. I left the police station, confident in the knowledge that common sense would prevail, but nevertheless phoned back some time later for an update.

Words escape me to describe the scale of my shock and horror when I discovered that not only had Mr S not been assessed by a psychiatrist, but he had also been granted bail and was gone!

My job was to get the best result for my client, and there could be no disputing that he would have been elated to be set free, but bloody hell! I received an email from my dear brother a few days later. It read:

'Hi Butt,

Mum told me about the case. I just wanted to express my admiration for your advocacy skills and wonderment at their sufficiency to restore an axe murderer to the streets.

May I temper my applause, though, with a small word of caution. If I am ever promenading through Stratford Park minding my own business, and I happen upon an armed Mr S; Mr S identifies me as an unbeliever and I, by chance or good fortune, happen to survive, I am coming round to kick your arse!'

## Rocket Man

It looks like I have been sacked by Mr L and will now have to break this news to my supervising solicitor.

Mr L fancied himself as a designer, although his drawings were of a standard that would make a five-year-old's sketches of mummy and daddy and a bus actually look like mummy and daddy and a bus. Admiring his picture of a space rocket, complete with seats reserved for all his friends including the privileged yours truly, I had the audacity to suggest that concrete might not be the best material for construction. I was only trying to help and personally thought that Mr

L's hostility in response was beyond all sense of proportion. The stick man bearing my name located amidships but enjoying a private window was callously struck out with a red pen by my client who, unblinking and with gritted teeth, simultaneously stared me down. He dispensed with my legal services too, which was arguably equally, if not more, disappointing.

## Shrunken Head

Mr B laboured under the unshakeable delusion that during a particular flight from Africa the pilot had managed to co-ordinate the shrinking of his head. All conventional therapy seemed to be failing. The one thing that Mr B wanted more than anything was to confront the pilot about the evil that had been put upon him.

I saw a letter in the file. My supervising solicitor had traced and written to the pilot, duly setting out the circumstances of the complaint and respectfully requesting a meeting with the patient. Disappointingly, the pilot had politely declined. I speculated that the pilot, fearing that the authorities might be on to him for shrinking a passenger's head without consent, wished to lie low.

I read the exchange in complete bewilderment. Who needed the therapy more, Mr B or my supervising solicitor?!

## Time to Say Goodbye to Mental Health and Hello To Qualification

I undoubtedly enjoyed my time in the mental-health

department but had spent more time in psychiatric hospitals than most patients. In the way that being a doctor surely makes one more aware of one's own mortality, similarly, spending so much time with those mentally unwell made me vulnerable to the realisation that I, too, was not so far removed from a disordered mind as I would have been comfortable with. It scared me.

I felt quite disturbed by the whole environment and, deep down, terribly sad for those having found themselves battling a mental illness as well as having to deal with the loss of their liberty. I would go as far as to say that my witnessing young people in particular, tormented by their thoughts and confined to an austere therapeutic regime, caused me deeper regret than anything I experienced in my criminal practice. I knew I was serving an important function, but a new chapter awaited, returning to crime as a fully-qualified solicitor.

# Back to the Fold

At long last I was qualified and proudly hung my practising certificate on the wall. I continued to share a room with James, who had also now qualified. The aim now was to generate our own caseload rather than work on other people's cases.

It was soon apparent that I would struggle to maintain a large enough caseload to hit my endless costs targets, which was imperative to avoid the wrath of the bosses. Organisation and efficiency in administration, essential to the task, were not my strong points. Working and talking enterprisingly to get a client off a charge, however, was.

A good many solicitors were very efficient case handlers but shied away from court advocacy. Those proficient in court advocacy tended to shy away from case handling, not least because they had little time due to their court commitments. There evolved a kind of team for each camp.

I was one of the guys who would spend his life in court mainly conducting the trials on cases prepared by the other solicitors. The costs attributed to a fee earner in any particular case were assessed on a percentage basis of work done. Of course, each solicitor wanted to maximise his or her costs so as to hit targets and earn bonuses, and they were quick and without shame in deploying themselves to do so.

By way of illustration, let us say that a complete case was worth £2,000 to the firm. I might spend a day in court doing the difficult stuff, such as the trial. Had the solicitor spent the equivalent time preparing the case, then the costs of the case would be attributable on a fifty per cent basis; £1,000 towards my target and £1,000 towards hers. We both get a pat on the back. The ploy, though, was for the caseworker to bill more time on the case and accordingly diminish my percentage whilst increasing hers. Every time she makes a coffee, has a poo or calls her husband, she will bill time for 'perusing the file', 'researching law', 'scheduling statements' or 'reflecting upon the evidence'. Suddenly she has billed twenty-five hours of work to my five. My proportion of the costs is now £400 to her £1,600. She gets a bonus, I get an arse-lashing. I think they call it capitalism, folks!

Costs-related whippings were variously dished out to all members of the advocacy team. They were largely sadistically motivated and gratuitous because, cynically, the bosses knew that the whole costs attribution wheeze was fundamentally unfair. The court hearings were integral; good results in court resulting in repeat clients, the economics of which were trickier to quantify. If flogging the mule somehow resulted in another penny for their coffers, though, then so much the better.

I tried to keep my head below the ramparts as much as possible, but with limited success. Jo, a member of the advocacy team and the most gifted courtroom advocate that one could hope to encounter, tended to get it in the neck more than most. He invariably got every accused person off everything they were ever accused of, assisted in large part by his charming manner and exquisite command of the English language, but that did little to prevent him being a target. His monthly costs figures were abysmal. If not in court he could usually be found secreted away in his little room, feet up on the table, eyes closed, listening to opera, his preferred entertainment and a subject in which he even had a university degree.

On one conspicuous occasion the bald-headed, bearded and portly figure of Jo was observed to shuffle hurriedly past my office hotly pursued by 'Make Yourself Indispensable', who, it appeared, was demanding an explanation for the discourteous failure to respond to the email concerning his lamentable costs total. On further investigation it emerged that not only had Jo failed to read a single email for the preceding three years, he had not even switched his computer on, being insufficiently inspired to do so. Such was the immeasurable exasperation and feeling of helplessness of the senior powers that they largely, thereafter, threw their hands in the air and left him alone to listen to his opera and win the occasional trial at court. I just wish the same mercies had been extended to me.

## New Clients

Quite regularly a new client would walk in off the street and reception would phone round the office in an attempt to get someone to see them. It generally meant dropping everything else that you were doing, when there was never enough time anyway, seeing the client and then dealing with all the resulting admin. I was never keen, my preference being for a trainee or paralegal to oblige and then open the case for another, more diligent, solicitor. Occasionally I could either not think up an excuse fast enough, had recently been admonished for my poor costs figures, or both, and was therefore forced to grudgingly agree.

## Wanker

I saw Mr R in the conference room located just to the left of the glass-fronted reception area. The conference room had two entrances, one for the general public and one for staff. It worked a little like an airlock, preventing the infiltration of hoodlums and rapscallions into the main network of offices.

Mr R had been charged by the police with exposing himself in a public place. He was a young man of twenty-two who impressed upon me firmly that this was nothing more than a clear case of mistaken identity. He appeared to be a genuinely decent guy, a man of the utmost integrity, committed to his girlfriend and a devoted father to their young baby. I was convinced by his account and felt sympathy that someone so obviously innocent should be accused of such scandal.

'Oh, before you go,' I said, 'do you have any previous convictions?'

I flicked through his case papers to the record of antecedents. He had an unblemished record, save for his twelve previous convictions for flashing...

## Tasty Turkish Kebabs

I have always mused that any food establishment that describes itself as 'quality' probably isn't. I would naturally assume quality to be implied; an expression of the same in the very name of the place would be superfluous to requirements, surely? It is a bit like protesting too much. The same principle goes for the 'Tasty Turkish Kebab Shop' in East 13, London, a somewhat untidy outlet where dining success is measured in inverse proportion to the resulting dysentery. Tastiness is of relative insignificance.

A very nasty incident had occurred there a week prior to the time I sat with Mr H in the office, a person the police held responsible for the unpleasantness. And they were soon to invite the magistrates' court to do the same.

Mr H told me what had happened: As is common knowledge, salad in a kebab is put there for one purpose, and that is to decorate the pavement. Perish the thought that a person might actually eat the stuff in real life. Nobody could criticise Mr H, then, for his act of ceremonial salad dumping.

He could have been a little more discerning about the area in which he discarded the tomato, though. Had he been, he may never have slipped; indeed, had the rotating doner kebab meat been a little more substantial, then his forward momentum might have been effectively arrested. It was just bad luck that the full thirty kilograms of greasy meat hit the deck. The defence to count one, criminal damage, was therefore one of 'accident'.

As both he and the tomato continued on their trajectory, Jayne Torvill-style, he 'bumped into' the proprietor causing him to suffer the injury that we could see in the photographs. In answer to count two, causing grievous bodily harm with intent, once again, the defendant averred 'accident'.

Making it clear that I wasn't prejudging the veracity of his account, I had one or two questions for Mr H to prepare him for the sort of interrogation that a prosecutor might undertake at trial:

1. 'The doner kebab was two metres away, on the other side of the counter. How, pray, did you have cause to 'steady' yourself on the kebab, unless you had hurdled the four-foot-high counter?'

2. 'How did the proprietor lose his hand? Was that anything to do with the kebab knife shown on the CCTV footage to be in your possession?'

3. 'How did the place burn down and what was your defence to count three, "arson"?'

He seemed to think that he might be in some difficulties after all.

'I am going to have to plead guilty, aren't I?' he asked.

'Yep.'

It is as a footnote to this reminiscence that I have to say as a generic, one-size-fits-all defence 'I slipped' takes some beating. When I finally come to leave this game, which will doubtless be with a shove, moments after this book is published, I vow to run this defence in every one of my remaining cases:

'You broke the window.'

'I slipped.'

'You ran over the policeman.'

'I slipped.'

'You tossed off the alpaca.'

'I slipped.'

# Up Before the Beak

Every morning was now spent at some magistrates' court goodness knows where in London or Essex. I would invariably have multiple cases to deal with in various courtrooms covering the whole spectrum of the different types of hearing. I may have three or four trials a week too. There was never time to prepare cases properly and so the ability to think on one's feet was a skill urgently acquired.

For my first few trials I would spend days preparing, writing out every question for cross-examination and every word of my speech, but what with the huge time pressures and stacks of cases, that didn't last for long. With increasing frequency, I would read the case for the first time on the tube to court and scribble something on the back of a fag packet as an *aide-memoire*. Either oratorical pearls would cascade from my lips or I would be struck dumb through lack of preparation. Either way, it all added to the fun.

It wasn't long before I became well acquainted with the district judges in the local courts. While the most noteworthy, and at times terrifying, idiosyncrasies of personality seemed to be the preserve of the crown court judges, there were also a good number of interesting district judges. The reputation of some preceded them, and not for characteristics of enduring compassion and indulgence I can tell you. The notorious and ominously-dubbed 'Custody Carson' being one and 'She whose name I dare not speak' another. You would know if she was due to preside that day by the presence of a special chair behind the bench, wheeled out for 'Her Excellency's' delicate behind. It had a high back and a head rest that was presumed necessary to brace against her frenzied rages triggered by nefarious occurrences, such as a solicitor being a second late for court, or breathing air. You didn't actually need to see 'the death chair' to know that she was sitting that day. The series of 'fucks', 'oh fucks' and 'bollocks' as successive solicitors filtered into court before you in the early morning was sufficient to alert you to the fact that you were probably going to have a bad day.

## The Adventures of Pee Man

Whilst the measure of success for the majority of my court days was mere survival until 4.30pm, occasionally I would come away having thoroughly enjoyed myself, or at least with a deep sense of gratitude that I was me, and not the person I was representing. On this occasion I happened to be representing a gentleman accused of distributing pornographic videos.

With changing public attitudes to sex and pornography, I suspect that today, the material which formed the subject of the charges would be viewed as comparatively tame and get nowhere near a court. Back then, they were considered capable to 'deprave and corrupt' and as such transgress the Obscene Publications Act of 1959.

Court hearings command solemnity, but nobody, including the court clerk, district judge, court usher and all those sitting in the public gallery could muster a straight face when this charge sheet was read out aloud.

It read as follows: You have been charged with publishing an obscene article, a video, contrary to Section 2 of the Obscene Publications Act 1959 namely:

*The Adventures of Pee Man.*

*Hair Today, Gone Tomorrow.*

*Shaving Ryan's Privates.*

*Shagtanic* (when the boat hits the iceberg everybody goes down).

*Cross-Channel-Ferry Sluts Take It Up the Arse, Part 5* (I think you needed to watch the first four to be able to follow the storyline).

*Back-Door Mania 2000.*

*Winnie the Pork.*

*Edward Penis Hands.*

*Raiders of the Lost Arse.*

*Willie Wanker and the Chocolate Factory.*

*Night of the Giving Head.*

*Saturday Night Beaver.*

*Anus the Menace.*
*Honey, I Blew Up My Tits.*
*Best Rears of Our Lives.*
*Throbbin' Wood.*

## I Thought It Was a Trumpet and Played a Tune On It

I had considered the defence in this case to be, for want of a better description, utter bollocks, the expression 'caught red-handed' being particularly apposite. A guilty plea ahead of the trial date entitles a defendant to a reduction from his or her sentence. The aim is to encourage guilty pleas and save the justice system the time and expense of trying those who are prepared to admit that they have committed the crime. This is what I felt should have happened here, but my 'firm advice' to the client for weeks along the lines of 'stop being a fucking idiot and plead guilty' was rebuffed, forcing me to endure this fandango.

For those who don't know, a 'glory-hole' is the colloquial name given to a circular aperture bored through the wall of two adjoining lavatory cubicles into which one, if so inclined, may insert one's penis. Both the one doing the inserting and the recipient in the adjacent cubicle can then engage in joyful acts, heightened, one may assume, by the enchantment of anonymity.

So it was that when security kicked open the lavatory door at the local sports club my client was sat on the bog, large Italian salami in his hand and a face like a plasterer's radio. It was my humble view, given that the scene disclosed pretty compelling evidence of some prior concerted genital husbandry, that the case was rather a strong one.

And it was for this reason that, had my client had access to a penis on that morning in court, I might have invited him to play the funeral march on it, such was the sombre mood as we reluctantly prepared to articulate his ludicrous defence.

Under oath, he explained to the justices, as he had to me, that, whilst he was in the process of discreetly evacuating his bowels, a penile intruder had appeared suddenly through the hole in the partition. Motivated by horror, and shock at the audacity, he indignantly (also rhythmically, one might suppose) struck the penis in the hope that it might be swiftly retracted. At the same time, he reinforced his efforts with the austere command, 'Be gone with you, I say!' The notion that he had deliberately stimulated the appendage, he told them, was an appalling affront to his moral values and high rank within the parish council.

In my closing speech, I gave the justices my time-hallowed 'we all know this is bollocks, but I have to do my job,' look. I then threw in a bit of Shakespeare for no reason other than to be facetious: 'What man dare, I dare. Approach thou like the rugged Russian bear?' and 'Wilt thou be gone? It is not yet near day./It was the nightingale, and not the lark,/That pierced the fearful hollow of thine ear', and gazed wistfully into the yonder.

The justices gawped at me as if I had gone perfectly insane (I probably had) before retiring. I slouched in a chair at the back of the court to await the inevitable conviction – a conviction that never came.

What followed was an emphatic, 'Not guilty.' The justices mused, what would the world be like if one were not at liberty to assert oneself and oppose the trespasses from another's trousers? They even commended my client for his bravery, as did I subsequently, and in the most sincere way I could summon. I apologised to him for my misplaced scepticism, if I had ever given the impression that his demonstrably honest account might have been horse shit.

## In Shit Street

It was quite a novel approach, I thought, for my client to suggest that tossing glass milk bottles full of his excrement across the road and onto a neighbour's doorstep could amount to an act of reasonable self-defence. There was certainly no denying what had happened. One just needed to cross reference the photograph of him complete with bottle of shit in hand, to the subsequent photographs of the neighbour's front door covered in shit and fragments of broken glass.

By this time in my career I was proficient in adapting my demeanour to the prevailing climate, but it appeared that the young woman prosecuting was unfortunately less able. Her mid-trial fit of the giggles became so entrenched, assisted in small part by my earnest imploring of her to take such grave matters more seriously, that the chairman erupted, slammed his papers on the bench and left the court until 'she' could 'bloody well pull herself together'. Have you ever seen a teacher successfully imploring a pupil to stop laughing in circumstances that demand solemnity? You get the picture, poor woman.

## Piss-Poor Preparation Equals Piss-Poor Performance

I have heard of 'fat cat' lawyers, but they certainly do not work in crime, either as solicitors or barristers. Criminals clever enough to pay their lawyers are also clever enough not to get caught; the rest need legal aid, and legal aid does not pay well. The only way to earn anything approaching a reasonable living from legal aid is to pile the cases high and work quickly.

The courts also try to dispose of as many cases as quickly as they possibly can. For me, one of my biggest bugbears of court practice was preparing for trials only to find that I was listed behind five others and had no prospect of being called on. The court's ploy, and indeed one adopted habitually by the crown court too, was to list too many trials to be dealt with. If one trial should not proceed, be it due to witness difficulties, late guilty pleas, disclosure arguments, or whatever, there would be another trial to take its place meaning that a trial court would never stand empty. The convenience to the court staff and 'efficiency statistics' assumed priority over everything else. There appeared to be an attitude of complete indifference to the time spent preparing the case by the lawyers, the waiting around at court while other work was neglected back at the office, and the inconvenience caused to witnesses who would have to return on another day.

It is little wonder then that intrinsic to magistrates' court practice was the lack of preparedness that flowed from a multitude of factors including the daily overload of work. On any one day I would expect to attend court with armfuls of case files representing the full spectrum of hearings from first appearances to sentencing. Invariably, the case files had been managed by other solicitors but even in the unusual circumstances of one of them being mine, I would still generally have no clue what was going on.

Of an evening, trying to read the cases and decipher what had gone on before, and what needed to be done, was a forensic and time-consuming operation. Planning how to survive the court day without a serious complaint from a judge or client demanded artistry. I, like most other solicitors I knew, relied on the train journey to court, time between cases, and expertise in 'winging it' to see me through.

On one particular trip to West London Magistrates Court with five cases in hand, I had cause to represent a young man on a charge of non-domestic burglary. He had pleaded guilty, and I stood up on his behalf in order to plead mitigation of his sentence, which I did very ably I thought. I explained how he had really turned his life around, turned his back on acquisitive offending, and was resolved never to find himself on the wrong side of the dock, or a stranger's front door, again. I thought that a sentence of four months' imprisonment was a splendid result for him considering his previous convictions and the nature of the offence. I made the same observation to him in the cells before leaving court.

It was only when writing up my attendance notes on the journey home that I identified the not insignificant blunder I had made. I had got my files mixed up and this gentleman had been up for an assault, not burglary at all. His actual previous convictions, and not those of some stranger to which I had referred, showed that he had never stolen anything in his life! Such was the overburdened, chaotic and fast pace of the magistrates' courts that nobody had listened to me sufficiently or, if they had, no one had cared sufficiently to point out my error. It was nevertheless a reasonably lenient sentence for the offence with which he had been charged, so it was probably best just to keep shtum. Goodness knows what my burglar client thought when I spent twenty minutes telling the magistrates what a thoroughly honest fellow he was and how he regretted beating up his girlfriend!

In life, whenever a dark cloud looms, it is nice to know that somebody else is in deeper strife than you are. Generally, that was the mantle held by the prosecutor, who would almost certainly have the full court list to prosecute and be under even more pressure than you.

I was reflecting on this when representing a client of mine up for yet another shoplifting trial. Reading a case five minutes before the hearing is one thing, reading it for the first time when on your feet is another. Having read not a bean prior to the commencement of the trial, the prosecutor, in his haste, read aloud the entirety of a police officer's notebook without having taken the time to edit out anything irrelevant. I can't deny my enjoyment at observing his duteous fluency stumble over endless references to my client 'busting for a crap', 'absolutely busting for a crap' and 'going to shit his pants if they didn't let him go'. This lasted until the chairwoman, distinguished by her courtly manner, reverence and being somebody less likely to deliberately pass wind in public than Her Majesty the Queen, begged him to stop.

## Shellfish Cunt

My client was adamant that he had not referred to a member of the local constabulary as a 'shellfish cunt'. He couldn't see any reason for it. It was true that he possibly despised seafood even more than he did the police but, nevertheless, he denied calling anyone a 'shellfish anything' despite his antipathy towards the *fruits de mer*.

True to form, the 'victim', PC Plod, told the court that, whilst he could not recall the specifics of the event due to the passage of time, if it was written in his police notebook, there could be no room for doubt. The magistrates announced that they were satisfied beyond all reasonable doubt that the assertion of the officer must be correct; he was a police officer, after all. There was plainly no reasonable possibility that this was a typo. After two hours discussing 'shellfish cunts', one poor joke about the 'scales of justice', and to my client's utter bewilderment, he was duly convicted and given a community punishment order. Thankfully, he wasn't that fussed after some consolation. Whether 'selfish' or 'shellfish', he was going to be picking up litter and painting fences regardless.

## High-Speed Pursuit

Sometimes the manner in which witnesses describe an unpleasant event really conjures up an image in one's mind. I have no idea what the police officer had said to my client Mr K to aggravate him so, but the provocation was enough to excite the wheelchair-bound Mr K into violently attacking him. Police officers are usually robust characters, but this one recalled from the witness box how he had felt so intimidated by Mr K that he thought it best to run off, not appreciating how keenly Mr K would pursue him. At some point both parties ended up on a busy highway with the valiant law-enforcement officer hard on his toes, but with Mr K gaining ground. The officer recounted how, due to the high-speed nature of the chase, Mr K's chair wobbled and then tipped, spilling the belligerent Mr K onto the road and almost causing a serious collision between an articulated lorry and a Ford Fiesta. Even the police helicopter was diverted to the location as Mr K continued to spit venom and vitriol from the central reservation of the A406.

## Pungent Offence

By the time of this case, I had conducted hundreds of magistrates' trials and was getting more than a little bored and restless. I had very little appetite to go to Thames Magistrates Court to defend somebody for failing to provide a specimen of breath on a good day. And this wasn't one. The only thing that made it a little more bearable was the nature of the defence.

Upon being stopped by the police on suspicion of drink-driving, and being demonstrably pissed, Mr B pleaded a lung condition to explain the insufficiency of his specimen of breath at the roadside. He did the same at the police station when they invited a further test in the 'intoximeter' room. Not once did he mention the reason that he now proffered, that he was gripped by chronic diarrhoea and would surely have an accident should he so much as think about exhaling into the machine. He explained to me, and indeed to the incredulous district judge, that he had failed to tell the 'truth' to the police at the time of the event purely out of embarrassment. Fortuitously, he had grown in confidence in the past month to the degree that he was now able to describe his leaky bowels to a packed courtroom.

It was obvious from the outset that his trial was perfectly doomed and that it was a case of going through the motions – no pun intended. I did take objection, though, to the bellicosity of the judge, who had appeared unimpressed by my respectful retort to his enquiry about medical evidence that there was probably little a doctor could do other than present a skidmark in Mr B's underpants marked as Exhibit A.

Neither were the judicial hostilities abated by my presentation of the key defence exhibit, a photocopy of a white porcelain lavatory. My client had handed me the photograph believing that it might have some relevance, but without any explanation as to why. One might have thought that my client was just trying to have a joke, but actually he was completely serious, just mad. Unperturbed,

I handed the picture to the judge with a swagger more consistent with my having revealed a smoking gun than a badly photocopied depiction of an enamelled crapper.

My case rested with one final, respectful suggestion, that Mr B not simply be acquitted for lack of credible prosecution evidence, but rather applauded for his steadfastness in avoiding a pungent offence within the confines of the police station.

The conviction that followed ten seconds later was not the problem; that was an inevitability. The problem lay in the kind invitation from His Worship for a post-trial meeting in his room. An attempt to decline on the basis that I was not partial to tea and a custard cream did nothing to 'improve the cut of my jib' apparently, so I proceeded unenthusiastically through the door at the back of the court for the admonishment of my life. The judge even had the brass neck to suggest that I hadn't taken the case seriously!

There then followed the first formal letter of complaint to my firm by a judge. A miracle, frankly. By rights, I should already have had about forty by then.

## No Wigs in the Magistrates' Court

As you know, there are no wigs and gowns in the magistrates' court. Those persons who enjoy dressing up in fancy dress as much as they admire the sound of their own voices are best encouraged to conduct their theatrics within the grand surroundings of the crown court. Unfortunately for her, a young pupil barrister who strolled past a colleague and me in the court foyer was firmly of another view. She proceeded assuredly, head held aloft, decorated with a bright, white wig and wearing a new gown, ready for her first ever court hearing. My colleague, a more sympathetic and generally nicer person than me in every respect, decided that it was only kind to correct her error, lest there be any further humiliation. Upon doing so the pupil barrister reacted with a good measure of scorn.

'I have been told about people like you!' she said.

She then stomped off to court. Whoever it was that had stitched her up had done an admirable job of it. I wondered if she had remembered to take with her a bucket of steam, left-handed hammer, tin of stripy paint and some sky hooks, too.

## BAN/1

Evidence is displayed in essentially two forms: witness statements and exhibits. A police officer, for example, may create a witness statement attesting to his discovery of the shotgun during the course of a search. The shotgun itself would be an exhibit. If the officer was called Smith, then he might label the shotgun exhibit SMI/1. The wraps of crack cocaine that he also unearthed during the search would be an exhibit, too. They would be given a separate exhibit number, such as SMI/2, and so on.

All prosecution material is disclosed to the defence at an early stage of proceedings. This is a fundamental rule of criminal practice designed to prevent ambushes and to allow the defence to properly develop their case. A defence case file, then, would be divided up into sections: compartmentalising the witness statements and copies of the exhibits. In theory, a separate section for the material gathered by the defence would also be created, along with one for unused material. In reality, by the time of the trial, the file would have been through so many hands, and kicked around a floor or filing cabinet for so long, that any earlier attempt at organisation would, by then, be a distant memory. Chaos reigned supreme.

Idling one day at the photocopier, I decided, as one does, to photocopy the banana that I had in my hand. There was no reason to do so; it was mindless, but it momentarily lightened the accursed boredom that flowed from time spent in the office. It was then that I was struck with an exceptional idea.

I would label my new document as 'Exhibit BAN/1', take multiple copies, and then secrete them into the exhibit bundles of files all around the office. I chose cases where a banana might have been consistent with a theme: offensive weapons, assault, robbery, indecent exposure, to name but a few. It tickled me to think that the new 'exhibits' would be happened upon by solicitors in inopportune moments, doubtless causing them perturbation followed by vexation at the question of which puerile individual was responsible. That question would likely not detain them for long, actually, but, regardless, a grand plan it was indeed.

The botheration that did come to pass was that, having spread the new 'evidence' to the four quarters, and particularly after the passage of a few days, I had no idea where the 'exhibits' had all gone. With no way of tracing them among thousands of messy solicitors' files, I had no way of rediscovering those bad eggs for potential retrieval if ever I had a change of heart. And the one thing likely to precipitate a change of heart, is the thought that circumstances may intervene.

The ill-advised acts of sabotage were all but forgotten until some two weeks or so later when Sandra, one of the solicitors, entered my room. Did I know anything, she enquired, of a banana exhibit within her evidence bundle in the assault case of D? The senior district judge had happened upon it during the course of the trial, she said, sparking an intense debate between lawyers and the police officers. Further enquiries were made back at the police HQ, but before it was decided conclusively that the article must have been a fake, the defendant, who had a diagnosed mental disorder, had experienced a form of catastrophic breakdown as a result. He believed that the manipulation of evidence was further proof of a persecutional state conspiracy against him. The only option available to the judge was to abort the trial at huge expense, seek medical assistance for the accused and then smoke out the justice-perverting wretch responsible for the outrage. In the first instance, an invitation is given to the culprit to come clean, to write a letter of explanation. Should the offender continue to lie low, further action may be taken.

Holy Shit!!!!

I gazed at her in disbelief before my mind turned rapidly to the question of evasion, and the best way to take it. An initial denial, consistent with my natural bias towards foul means rather than fair in times of trouble was, on further consideration, unlikely to wash. A short pause for reflection foretold an internal investigation so expansive and unceasing that I simply didn't have the pluck or fortitude to ride it out. Cornered and conflicted in my judgement, I came clean, to Sandra's apparent shock.

'I am sorry,' she said. 'It's now over to you.'

Immediately, I wrote a long, grovelling letter of apology to the judge and threw it in the first-class post, just in time for it to get out that evening. It was inevitable that the partners would find out and I would certainly lose my job, but any remote chance to avoid that, was one I had to take. The next week was spent searching every single file, in every single filing cabinet, in every single office after work in the hunt for BAN/1s. I would stay in the office until the early hours of the morning, thinking of and doing nothing other than hunting down those hideous bananas. I searched countless boxes of papers, hundreds of files and millions of pages. Terrifyingly, by the end of a tenacious mission, there were still a great many bananas unaccounted for; neither had I heard back from the judge. Anxiety was, by then, well established, and sleep a distant memory.

When the trawl was over, just when I was on the point of completely losing my mind, Sandra invited me out for a sandwich with the other solicitors and trainees. It was then that she confessed that she had been pulling my plonker the whole time, as had all the other attendees, who had conspired in the plan to get revenge for my endless 'dicking around and general skivery', as she described it. There had been no trial, no investigation and most concerning of all, no requirement for a letter of apology.

I crumpled into my chair, head in my hands.

What of the letter I sent to the judge? Goodness only knows what he made of that! I never heard a thing. Still, I would surely owe him an apology for something in the future, he could have that one on credit.

## Pastures New

A few years in the magistrates' court had caused me to grow a little weary. I was tired of the rules of evidence being misinterpreted or flouted and having to absorb badly-reasoned arguments advanced by both my opponent and lay benches of magistrates. It is enormously frustrating after years of training to make a well-researched argument, possibly very important to the case, only to lose that argument through the complete idiocy of a layperson, now appointed judge. Often it seemed that the verdict would just reflect the gut feeling of the tribunal and bear little relation to the quality of the evidence.

District judges were little better. At best they would be case-hardened, at worst, vindictive. All too often, they laboured under an assumption of guilt rather than working from a presumption of innocence, as the law prescribes. They were also often impatient and abrupt.

One case that really sticks with me is that of a woman who, in the presence of a police officer in her home, retrieved a knife from a kitchen drawer and, whilst severely depressed, ignored the demand of the police officer to drop it. She instead chose to cut her own wrists, such was the desperate state she found herself in. She was charged, spuriously in

118

my view, with threatening a police officer, something she had obviously not done. To add insult to injury, the district judge seemed to delight in convicting her, without any basis that I could see other than one which could only have been perverse. It upset and frustrated me hugely.

Examples like that were very common. People were getting convicted when they shouldn't have been. The evidence was not in a state to make a judge or magistrate sure of the defendant's guilt. There were even occasions when I saw people convicted of things that the evidence suggested they were demonstrably innocent of.

In a magistrates' court there is a single tribunal of law and fact, unlike in the crown court where the jury handle the facts and the judge the law. There is a risk that obvious injustices can result. If, during a trial, a magistrate or district judge hears an application to exclude evidence, and they agree, are they really going to be able to put the subject of that application from their minds? All sorts of underhand tactics could, and would, be employed by both the defence and the prosecution in making applications that were doomed to certain failure, but might nevertheless prejudice the bench in their favour.

There was a limit to the number of times I could come home, kick the cat and curse yet another flatulent, bearded, malignant dimwit for convicting someone who was quite possibly innocent. My tolerance was waning, as was my ability to remain courteous. The only positive thing I could do is that if there was ever a case that I really believed in, knowing that guilt rather than innocence was presumed, I would try very,

very hard. No stone would be left unturned and every tactic or technique for persuasion that I could muster would be deployed. When I came to practise in the crown court, where acquittals were altogether much easier to come by, I found as a consequence that I was habitually throwing atom bombs into cases where a subtle firecracker would have sufficed.

When Mrs S came into the office to see me I was well on the way to climbing the rungs into the crown court, but still had an endless list of magistrates' cases to get through. Mrs S told me that she intended to plead guilty to assaulting her husband and criminally damaging the wing mirror of his Jaguar. She explained how her husband had bullied her for years and that she had eventually snapped, hitting him with a frying pan and kicking off his wing mirror. From the way she described him, I was left with the firm opinion that her husband was an irredeemable nob.

Provocation is no defence in law to simple allegations of violence such as these and so, on paper at least, she probably was guilty. The red rag to the bull, though, was her cautioning me that her husband was a barrister, such a capable orator and wordsmith, that cross-examining him would be entirely futile. He would be all over me like a cheap suit and make the defence team look like sizeable tits.

There was no way that she would be pleading guilty now. I didn't care how guilty she was or what plea she wanted to enter, I wasn't having it. The gauntlet had been well and truly thrown down. In that one defining moment, the years of advocacy experience I had gained, the best parts of every question I had ever asked, every trap I had ever set, every bit of cunning, persuasion or chilling unpleasantness I had ever employed were exploited systematically with the aim of his undoing. By the time I had finished giving him such a thorough kicking, he didn't know who or even where he was.

The chairman of the magistrates appeared genuinely shocked to find himself in a position where he might actually go against his principles and find a defendant not guilty, especially in a case like this where cold application of the law to the facts might ordinarily dictate a fair finding of guilt. When the magistrates returned from their retirement, they found the defendant not guilty.

The elation of my client, and indeed my own, was celebrated with a lovely gift and card from her that I have treasured ever since. It was at this moment more than any other that I started to have ideas above my station, to think that my skills of persuasion were such that I could sell snow to Eskimos or leaf litter to 'El Chapo'.

When you believe that you can conquer the world you feel quite uplifted, and that confidence, in turn, made me a more convincing lawyer. It worked rather like an arse-blowing, smoke-recirculating device. I thought I could fly with the eagles. I had read that in the crown court the judges all apply the law correctly with an inherent sympathy towards the defence. There would be a jury of twelve laypeople, many seeing criminal cases for the first time, fresh, keen and without prejudices. The crown court was calling and I couldn't wait to be warmly welcomed and made to feel at home.

# Do You Have
# a Degree in Bar?

O f an evening, the court solicitors lined up in the
diary room, heads bowed, to be given their court
commitments for the following day. There would always
be some hearing in a far-flung court somewhere that the
partner, tasked with organising the diary, struggled to
cover. Convention would dictate a coincidental enquiry
about the whereabouts of Jo, our in-house and elusive
'crown-court advocate'. The boss's exasperated cries of
'pissing mention', suggested yet another swerving of the
real work of the magistrates' court in favour of something
undemanding in the crown court.

Jo, at that time, was what was once a rare breed of
lawyer called a 'higher court advocate'. They are a species
of criminal solicitor who, by reason of their significant
experience as such, were granted rights to practise in the
crown court. It was a requirement that a solicitor advocate
wear a gown conspicuously different from that worn by a
barrister and not very different from that of a court usher,

and also remain wigless. The result of all this was that solicitor advocates stood out like a fart in a lift and were about as well received. Solicitor advocates being made to look like idiots was, I am sure, all part of the defence against the threat they posed to the work of independent barristers.

By way of explanation, solicitors get the cases from the bottom, traditionally instructing barristers on the serious matters that go to the crown court. From time immemorial there have been these two tiers of the criminal legal profession with the business model relying on the premise that barristers receive their work from the solicitors. If solicitors could now instruct themselves on their own cases rather than give them to barristers, thereby gatecrashing the old boys' club, barristers had a problem. There isn't exactly a level playing field for work acquisition either; few barristers go to the police station or pick up cases as a duty lawyer.

And so there existed a general conspiracy at the crown court between judges and barristers, as I saw it, that operated to ensure that solicitor advocates were not made to feel too comfortable, to deter them from poaching.

Jo, at least, was sufficiently robust to be unfazed by the hostile milieu. He was so beaten down by his domineering wife that bullying by judges or barristers, however it manifested itself, was a picnic by comparison. The skill of his advocacy, too, appeared to impress and silence the embittered old boys of the bar.

By the time of my own pretentious imaginings, the route to becoming a solicitor advocate had recently changed. A series of courses and exercises rather than solely a history of court experience could enable one to become a solicitor advocate. My firm, made up largely of traditionalists, weren't very supportive of my lofty ambitions to be a crown court hero. I had little choice but to sneak off to a course, funding it myself. In keeping with their old-school ways, once I was qualified, they didn't support the idea of my conducting any crown-court work either, preferring instead to adhere to tradition. Jumped-up upstarts like me should know our place. All the more determined, I would creep off to conduct the court hearings on my own cases without telling a soul. My elusiveness clearly created an unwelcome mystery back at the office but by that time I was too resentful to care.

A solicitor advocate was a rare sight at the crown court back then, particularly one who was twenty-five years old, and no attempt was made to disguise the collective displeasure of the resident stiffs. I had a hell of a time: derided, belittled, patronised and humiliated endlessly by judges and barristers alike. One judge, for example, to the amusement of a packed courtroom, persisted in his insincere identification of me as a courtroom usher and not an advocate, owing to my garb. When counsel for the prosecution, enthusiastically joining in on the gag, haughtily informed His Greatness that I, in fact, appeared on behalf of the defence, the judge feigned huge astonishment, bellowed out some over-exaggerated guffaws and queried with other, apparently astonished court attendees whether what he had just heard could possibly be true.

On another occasion, a judge simply pretended that he couldn't hear a word I was saying, despite his hearing appearing perfectly in order when listening to the barristers. As I raised my voice, he continued to claim that he couldn't hear me. Perplexed, I was eventually advised by another attendee that crown court tradition dictated that if an advocate was dressed inappropriately, a judge would feign deafness until the distasteful blunder was corrected. By this stage in proceedings, especially considering the impudent little bastard I was back then, I was more than tempted to announce to the judge my opinion of him as an 'insufferable old cunt', before seeking gratitude for my help in curing his ailment, 'Yeah, you heard that, didn't you, you old bugger?' but I thought better of it.

After about ten minutes of this, playing the game as I I had to, I informed the judge what he already knew, that I was a solicitor advocate. This immediately prompted the question as to whether I had a 'degree in bar'. I was unable to answer the question as I had no idea what a 'degree in bar' was. Subsequent research revealed that there was no such thing, but that didn't prevent the judge from adjourning my ten o'clock case to the end of the day for me to provide him with a satisfactory answer.

Of course, all of this did little to instil confidence in one's client. He, too, not unreasonably, started to think that he would rather just have a 'normal' barrister, not a representative who was getting all this flak. This was, of course, all part of the grand design to rid the court of impostors. There was no point getting ruffled or riled; I just made myself a little jar of IOUs and fought to be a better lawyer than they were. Nobody likes to be beaten by the underdog, and it made the deserved hiding from me all the more fun when the opportunity eventually did arise to give it to them. Back then, though, I was just itching to do my first trial.

I had been working on a case concerning the supply of crack cocaine and heroin and decided that I would see it all the way through. It was a serious case, likely to attract six years imprisonment or more for my client if the verdict was adverse, and unquestionably it was pure lunacy to take it on as a first case. Not that that was going to stop me.

On the morning of the trial, my phone rang endlessly with calls from the office trying to discover my whereabouts, doing little to calm my nerves. As the prospective jurors filed into court for selection, I had a profound sinking feeling, like a parachutist who has just jumped from the plane only to remember that his 'introduction to the parachute' course began the following day. It was too late now to admit that I was a fraud, as I felt myself to be, and retreat to Barking police station or Thames Magistrates' Court.

Against the odds, I found my feet quickly and the trial progressed as smoothly as I could have hoped. Debatably, I even did a half-competent job; I wasn't even distracted by the female police officer's good looks. In fact, I gave her a particularly hard time in the witness box, remarking on the porosity and poverty of her investigation. I articulated publicly my displeasure at her amateurish inquiry, letting her know that it was as much of a disgrace as an incorrect verdict based on it would be. Her opposition, in return, was unmerciful, making little secret of the fact that she detested me on sight and displaying loathing for my effrontery before the jury. She made no apology for our exchange, nor did I, at any point up until we retired to the privacy of my bedroom that same evening. She remarked, in private, that the unenlightened courtship display, as she considered the whole thing to have been was not a single-horse race; indeed, His Honour the Judge had also proposed a clandestine rendezvous on the quiet! It was more my obnoxiousness than refinement that struck her, leaving her with little choice but to accompany me home for a 'shag'. Her reasoning appeared somewhat obscure to me if I'm honest, but being someone who picks his challenges wisely, I was not minded to argue. My cross-examination of her had ended, there could be no prejudice to my client's interests in his lawyer examining the officer in the case with a little more scrutiny than the law might have envisaged. Besides, I had no intention of announcing the doings of the previous evening; all was fine and dandy.

What I had failed to appreciate in my romantic haste was the outside possibility that, by virtue of my courtroom con-artistry, not all of the jurors would see my client's obvious guilt. If at least three of them remained unpersuaded, the jury would be deadlocked. A deadlocked, or hung, jury would result in a retrial and, as fate would have it, that was precisely what happened. The jury could not agree, were discharged, and a new trial ordered.

I was now in a serious 'brown trouser' position, having to conduct a retrial in circumstances which required a professional attack on a person who, not long before, had been loosening the screws on my three-quarter divan. They call that a conflict of interest in the trade, and it was a serious one.

Lacking a large carpet to sweep the whole mess under, which threatened to shower my debut in something other than glory, I found salvation in the form of Jo, to whose unsympathetic ear I disclosed my situation. There were no promises against seductive predation upon the young witness to whom I had by then become quite partial, but he agreed to navigate the retrial, duly saving my butt for which I remain eternally grateful.

I still had to explain to the big cheeses back at the office where I had been for the past week, and why I was reckless enough to take on such a serious trial, especially without consulting them. Additionally, I was required to enlighten them, somehow, as to why I would have to recuse myself from the retrial. On a different topic, while I was at it, I was told it would be as good a time as any to explain why, the week before, I had penned 'the anus is on your shoulders' in a letter to an already irate Crown Prosecution Service (CPS) lawyer (entirely my secretary's fault – she had been directed to write 'onus'). I could also inform them, if I wouldn't mind, why, having penned 'the anus is on your shoulders', I asked to meet the, now incandescent and formally complaining, CPS lawyer at the 'dildo building'. (I had accidentally sent this message to the lawyer rather than my friend whom I'd planned to meet at the London's Gherkin building, 30 St Mary Axe.)

I don't know what came first, the fuel thrown on the fire or the fanning of the flames, but according to any analysis my time at the office was drawing to an end.

What came of my alleged drug-dealing client? For all of Jo's eloquent diction at the retrial, the new jury promptly convicted him. I was really sorry for the defendant; he was a nice guy, for a drug dealer, but savoured the knowledge that I had at least done better than Jo; an achievement I took great pleasure in reminding him of.

## I Crashed the Party

They say that there is no panic like you feel when you have got your head trapped in something. I largely agree with that, leaving aside the occasion I managed singlehandedly to collapse a fraud trial which, by then, had been running for two months, involved six barristers and had accumulated costs of several hundred thousand pounds.

If you have ever had the misfortune of being dragged out of a fully constituted school assembly in a headlock by the biology teacher on charges of highlighting the headmaster's scrotum with a laser pen, then I can say, on good authority, you have an idea of the experience.

When the judge sent the jury out in the middle of my defence speech because I had subverted one of his legal rulings and he wanted to invite submissions on this, the episode bucked the trend of my pushing my luck but getting away with it. I hadn't expressly intended to undermine the legal ruling before the jury, but the allegation that the same effect had been achieved by a devious sleight of hand, was probably well founded. I hadn't just sailed close to the wind this time; I had stopped and clicked the boat into reverse. Fearing the wrath of the other barristers for wasting two months of their lives, a wasted costs order and probable disciplinary proceedings, my urgent back-pedalling was admirable, but futile. The jury was not going to be brought back.

All credit to the judge, an act of mercy on his part saw me largely off the hook. Having simmered down a bit after a ten-minute coffee break, his ultimate take on matters mirrored the notion that trainee doctors will inadvertently kill a number of patients in the name of education. In the same vein, a young lawyer learning the ropes will inevitably bollocks up the odd case. As for the other barristers, aside from pointing out what a truly unmitigated tit I was, they came away relatively grateful that their clients had been granted a stay of execution, and they now had a plump eight-week retrial to place in their diaries.

## Baseball Bat Attack

One or two of the younger solicitors at the firm had decided to give me a chance; in other words, had thrown me a couple of cases to stop my whining. One of these cases was that of a seventeen-year-old lad who, alongside his brother, was alleged to have very seriously injured a person who already struggled with an array of physical and mental disabilities.

It was said by the prosecution that the two brothers had set upon the victim when he was out on an organised day-trip with his friends. There didn't appear to be any particular justification or provocation; with the use of a baseball bat and stick, the brothers had beaten the victim unconscious and caused him grave harm. The evidence against them was compelling.

To the extent that my role was to do my best for my client and that the best for him would be adjudged by the extent to which his continued incarceration could be limited, I was undoubtedly the right barrister for the job. He had zero morals; so did I.

Given that the evidence, on the face of it, suggested two assailants, I considered that the first necessary step was to resolutely throw my client's brother under the bus.

In criminal proceedings, when one defendant's case is run adversely to the benefit of another, we call it 'going cut-throat'. It is, for obvious reasons, a trial strategy that is unpopular with the people who find their throats being cut and their legal teams. Despite the pleas of the co-defendant's barrister to deal with the case in a more brotherly and sympathetic way, I was unapologetically unobliging. If the most likely route to victory caused blood to be spilt, then spilt it would be. I proceeded to besiege his client ruthlessly in the witness box much to the horror of those representing his interests.

Having accounted for the presence of one attacker, all that was left was the identity of the other. This quandary was addressed with the use of some fancy footwork. I persuaded the jury that, when one looked collectively at the slight variations in descriptions proposed by various witnesses against clothing seized from my client on arrest, they would be unable to exclude the possibility that there had been in fact three men at the scene, rather than two. To follow the reasoning to its natural conclusion, if one attacker was the brother and the other one either my client or an unknown person, the jury was duty-bound to find my client not guilty on the basis that they would not be able to discern to the requisite standard of proof which one.

I hadn't called my client to give evidence before the jury. Not calling a defendant to testify in his own defence is a perfectly permissible tactic, and while there are many reasons consistent with innocence for taking this decision, none applied here. I didn't call him to the witness box purely and simply because I felt it unhelpful to impress upon the jury just what a lying, unpleasant and objectionable individual he truly was. He would also likely tell the jury that there were, in fact, only two persons at the scene and no mystery third male, the possibility of which I hoped might beguile the jury to my client's benefit.

The brother was convicted and received nine years' imprisonment. My client got off.

I went to see him in the cells after the jury had returned their verdict, just as preparations were being made to release him back out into the community. He was mildly grateful for my efforts, I think, but exceedingly brash and conceited. Feeling for the first time an odd sensation within me, later discovered to be known as a conscience, I spoke a few words in an attempt to trigger some reflection by my client as to what I personally believed he had done to that victim. My words were just a waste of breath.

I returned to the office to receive ego-expanding adulation for having pulled out of a hat something which had been deemed irretrievable. But when all the noise and excitement, the clamour, the congratulatory remarks and the elation inherent in the 'win' ebbed away, I was left sitting in my tatty office opposite Dave's mini-market with nothing but my own thoughts. I had grabbed victory from the jaws of justice but what with the next case banging on everyone's door, nobody could give a shit about the one that went before, or even how mighty an appendage the successful advocate believed he possessed. That was the way of the game. Nobody really cares or remembers what you did, other than possibly the poor victim.

When I was five years old I once watched a girl at school taking ages meticulously peeling an orange over a dustbin. When she eventually finished, I walked over to her and without saying a word knocked her arm so that the orange fell into the bin. I don't know why I did it. I walked off and never apologised. I still feel terrible to this day, and yet here I was doing the very same thing on a grander scale, and being paid for it.

With maturity and experience came the realisation that when given the responsibility of power that can impact so significantly on people's lives, that power needs to be used humanely.

# Welcome to Chambers

I received a telephone call from Jo. He had long moved away from the solicitors' firm and was now practising as an independent barrister. We chatted about the moves I needed to make to follow in his footsteps, the plan being for him to give me a leg up into his chambers.

Barristers are generally self-employed and practise out of 'chambers'. Traditionally, chambers would be located off The Strand in an area of London called the Temple, opposite the Royal Courts of Justice, which houses the Court of Appeal. Even to this day, when a barrister is required to attend the Court of Appeal, he will refer to the occasion as 'a trip over the road', whatever his actual current physical location.

Importantly, chambers would also be located within the precinct of one of the Inns of Court, of which there are now four: Gray's, Middle Temple, Inner Temple and Lincoln's. Every barrister must be a member of at least one of them. They have supervisory and disciplinary functions but also provide libraries, dining facilities and professional accommodation. Each also has a church or chapel attached to it and is a self-contained precinct where barristers traditionally train and practise.

As curious a custom and as old-fashioned as it may seem, in order even to qualify as a barrister, it is a requirement to eat dinner at your chosen Inn of Court on at least twelve separate occasions. Often the dining sessions include the provision of legal lectures in furtherance of the education of the aspiring lawyer and all conducted within the splendour of a seven-hundred-year-old institution whose grand architecture smacks of historic opulence. The food can be quite scrummy to boot! Even now I will occasionally enjoy a working lunch at Lincoln's Inn within the oak-clad dining hall, adorned with ten-foot paintings of famous lawyers and judges of old. If so inclined I might entertain myself with the gory niceties of an old capital-punishment law report housed in the library where dusty books in their thousands tower up to the heavens, accessed via wrought-iron mezzanines and ladders on rails. It is all breathtakingly lovely and connotes the high society and wealth with which it was associated in times gone by.

So few of the commuters and tourists who hurry along The Strand and Fleet Street have any idea of the world that lies behind the unassuming black, iron-studded doors that open out onto the famous thoroughfare. Should one venture through them, a land opens up complete with parks, cathedral-like Inns of Court, red-brick chambers serviced by cobbled alleyways and gas lighting. It is akin to stepping into a time warp.

Barristers' chambers were originally a place where lawyers would lodge and from where they would operate. Whilst there are now chambers located all around the country and barristers do not tend to regard them as places of residence, the business structure has changed little in centuries. Chambers are essentially offices and a central hub for the practising barrister. Members of chambers pay a monthly 'rent' for the building and in return their names can be found neatly written on a board at the door, the longest standing member at the bottom and newest addition at the top.

Chambers are generally headed by an elected member and space is set aside within the building for the barristers' clerks. On the face of it, the clerks work for the barristers. They are their agents who book in and manage cases sent in for the barristers. They promote and market the barristers and chambers, and seduce the work-providing solicitors. They distribute the work that comes into chambers that has not already been assigned to any particular barrister by the instructing solicitor. They monitor and organise the court listings to ensure that cases are always covered for the next day. At the end of the case, the clerks will then bill it and chase the fees.

For their services, the clerks charge a percentage of the case fee, often around ten per cent. Considering the number of barristers in an average set of chambers and the collective turnover, clerks can do very well indeed.

Criminal clerks are inherently wily and cunning. It is a vocation traditionally bequeathed from father to son, a closed shop. Reputed to be linked historically and by family to the 'barrow boys' of East London, they, like us, are effectively salesmen, though their primary mission is to charm the solicitors whose hands feed us all. To a solicitor, criminal clerks are a delight: a best friend for whom nothing is too much trouble. When you work for them, though – hmm, a Freudian slip – when they work for you, they are an altogether different proposition. You are not now feeding them, they are largely feeding you. Conviviality quickly turns to disinterestedness; you are a cog in the machine and replaceable. If you are needed to go to Nottingham Crown Court for a pre-trial review, which would cost you more in train fares than the pittance you receive in fees, then you go. If you are compliant, then you will be thrown a bone or two. If you complain and make the clerks' job more difficult, then the next decent brief received into chambers will pass you by and will be given to Tom Smithers who did that bail app you swerved in Woolwich last month. The day you piss off the clerks is the day you go down to the job centre to sign on.

Of course, if you have a loyal following of solicitors who regularly instruct you and are responsible for a flow of cash through chambers, the warm hand of friendship with the clerks will surely be maintained for longer. Coming from a firm of loyal solicitors, as I did, and with the promise of instruction, I was welcomed into chambers courtesy of a small leg-up from Jo. A cursory enquiry as to my ability as a lawyer was a token gesture only and, following my reduced dining requirement at my Inn of Court in acknowledgement of my legal experience already gained, I was in. Gone were the days of job security and a modest monthly wage. I was now self-employed; if I didn't get cases, then I wouldn't eat and faced the very real possibility of losing the shirt off my back, something I later came rather close to. Right then, though, I had earned the enviable right to wear a curly wig constructed from a horse's arse and to be referred to as 'my learned friend'. That was cool.

I learnt pretty quickly the necessity of forging relationships with solicitors. Fanning lots of wind up the bottoms of those who might send in those coveted briefs, neatly bound up with pink string, was a central requirement and responsibility. As solicitors we all know that when we are met with broad smiles and warm handshakes at a chambers' summer garden party, the barristers are just skilfully disguising their utter contempt for us. We are not looking for new buddies, though; we just want to get pissed on the free champagne and munch the smoked salmon and caviar canapés before making our excuses and leaving for a bar in Shoreditch with our real friends. In return, we all promise to deliver the hosts lots of work that we know will never materialise.

As a barrister, I quickly forgot my roots and happily joined in the universal disdain of barristers for those smug, power-drunk solicitor toads. We would feign interest at their 'humorous' stories from the magistrates' courts whilst watching them swill down the expensive grog and grub that came directly from our own pockets. I speak for all barristers when I say that I wish that solicitors would save their breath and refrain from complimentary, habitual, yet vacuous promises of lucrative work in exchange for booze. We all know it is tripe, just as solicitors know that when I say, ' I am amazed that you got Mr Smith off! You are a genius' or, ' I am so excited that you are to become a mum, great news!' I genuinely couldn't give a shit and will certainly be scrolling my online dating matches at the urinal while debating with my barrister mate next to me how much longer we need suffer this torture before we can do a bunk.

The truth is that, while the work givers may have an inclination towards those providers of lavishness, it is the capability and willingness to assist them in maximising their returns, holding their hands, and doing as much as possible of the work that they should be doing themselves that translates into new instructions, not the miniature fish and chips or tempura prawn on a stick.

I played the game, got a steady trickle of work, at least in the first couple of years of tenancy and managed, just about, to keep the wolf from the door.

# City Breaks

The job is often a very lonely pursuit. Particularly when practising out of the London metropolis, friendly faces are few and far between. Unlike the office environment where you can bounce off your work colleagues after a trip to court, as a barrister, the environment is more hostile to the creation of pals. You may see people familiar to you on the court circuit, but everyone is so busy putting out their own professional fires that there isn't too much time for socialising. If they happen to be in the same case as you, then you will, in all likelihood, be fighting and falling out with them, sometimes professionally, sometimes personally, often both.

The culture of the bar was once to frequent a wine bar near chambers after the court day, coinciding with the trip back to chambers to collect the briefs for the following one. My experience of it, though, was that the drink and chat was invariably short-lived. The pressure was always on to swot up for the next day with little time remaining after the arduous journey on the tube back from the West End to whichever far-flung part of the city one lived in. In any event, with the introduction of digital cases, gone were the papers tied up with string and slung into the pigeon hole awaiting collection. A new day had dawned, dispensing with the need to attend chambers on a daily basis and simultaneously killing off the late afternoon jaunts to Daly's Wine Bar.

Particularly in the earlier years, travel all around the country for work was an imperative. The usual ritual was for all and sundry to assemble around the clerks' room at about five o'clock in the afternoon, although getting too close to the madness within would result in a kindly, 'Fuck off, sir', from one of the clerking team as he wrestled with the court diary. It was like bedlam: phones ringing endlessly, papers and documents littering the room and floating off in all directions, and fussed lawyers flying past. You would probably find one barrister looking flustered, worriedly opening old letters previously neglected at the back of his pigeon hole. Another would be in the corner reading a law book, while others would be on their phones, chatting, checking football scores or chipping paper balls with a cricket bat into a litter bin.

Jo would saunter in bemoaning something or other, perhaps the frequent and antisocial digestive exit timetabling of the 'squatter'. A squatter is a barrister affiliated with chambers but not a 'tenant'. A squatter does not pay rent, nor stand cap in hand for work, but instead uses chambers as a vehicle to manage his or her existing and established caseload. The person in question here, a not insubstantial young woman, habitually enjoyed the facilities located within the heart of the clerks' room at 5pm sharp. Most were too polite, or short of oxygen, to comment upon the stench that pervaded thereafter. Jo, on the other hand, would bound in ruddy-faced and spluttering to an awkward audience as to his apparent ability to 'cut the atmosphere with a knife', and how the lady was a 'squatter' for reasons far exceeding her unwillingness to contribute to the rent.

If you were lucky you might be lobbed a couple of bits at Snaresbrook Crown Court or Inner London the following day. If you were not, a trip to Wolverhampton, Nottingham or Stafford might be your unfortunate fate. If predicted to stay there for some time then, upon receiving your briefs, the rush was on to get home, throw some clothes in an overnight bag and attempt to get a train out that evening. Nothing would be booked for the night but the destination would be sure to offer some crappy hotel to stay in. Legal aid would be unlikely to pay for travel or hotel expenses, but if it did, £40 per night would be about your lot. At best this would buy you a night in a shithole; at worst, it wouldn't.

You might be given a stabbing, rape, or serious fraud trial, plus a load of other bits and pieces to juggle. In an ideal world, you would take a month to prepare it all. In the real world, though, you had the time it took to travel between London and whatever God-forsaken cesspit you were headed for to read a sufficient amount to wing it. The papers would always be a horrible mess; complete with indecipherable endorsements from previous counsel through whose hands the brief had passed and undoubtedly missing crucial documents. That is even before we get to the inevitable inadequacies of the work that had gone before. Just as it had been as a solicitor, the buck would stop with the last hot potato handler. Engrossed in the conundrum of how best to mitigate it, your head wouldn't lift once from the curled up bundles of pages sat in your lap as the English countryside chickety-chicked by, save possibly to react violently upon being run over for the third time by the extortionate drink-and-snacks trolley.

## Robin Hood

This shitty stick came in the form of a trip to Nottingham: less the home of Robin Hood and more the home of robbin' banks, it seemed. While London had its fair share of crime, Nottingham seemed to be in an altogether different league, taking its comparatively small size into account. I was given about five different cases a day to manage as well as an ongoing trial, all of which were of the utmost serious-ness. Thoughts of Sherwood Forest and quaffing ale in the oldest pub in England quickly gave way to the actuality of legal chaos: bad-tempered judiciary and lawyers racing from courtroom to courtroom followed by police officers clutching zip-tied evidence bags containing anything from class A drugs to sawn-off shotguns.

The usual checklist was ticked:

1. Carrier bag containing a toothbrush, odd socks and an insufficient number of pants to last two days let alone a week. Check.

2. Phone charger missing. Check.
3. Residence in a DSS bed-and-breakfast/brothel. Check.
4. Gross inadequacy of case preparation. Check.

The trip was ill-fated, as such trips always were, but I suspected that I would be able to bluster my way through just as I had always managed in the past.

Having found my way to the wretched crown court, late and sweating, I didn't exactly welcome the intrusive busybody that I encountered in the lift en route to the robing room.

'You should be wearing a tie in the crown court!' she scorned.

I generally pride myself on my courteousness, but today, anxious as I was to get to court, I scornfully dismissed her. What concern was it of hers anyway? Rumour had it that the judge in my courtroom was nothing short of evil and, if I didn't get to the robing room without delay to don my court garb and make a timely courtroom appearance, my arse would be grass, so to speak. There was no time for dilly-dallying: tying ties, prettying myself up and all that nonsense for the benefit of onlookers in the court foyer. Articulating my utter contempt for her objection, I retorted, 'I am late to a court appointment with Her Honour Judge Grotbags. She finds late attendees as objectionable as I do the suggestion that ties be worn on a boiling hot day in a crapped-out court foyer.'

The old dear silenced, I legged it off, changed into my collar, bands, wig and gown, and made it into court moments before the judge did.

'All Stand!' cried the court clerk.

We all stood up as we always do as a mark of respect to the judge as she strode in. She seemed immediately familiar to me, but I couldn't quite put my finger on it. Was it London? I hadn't been to Nottingham before. That would be a coincidence. Had I seen her somewhere today? The café? The court foyer? No, I didn't think so. Oh no, the lift? No! Please, no! Oh fuck! Fuck, fuck, fuck, bollocks, fuck!

Slinking under the bench, I would have made it clean below the surface had it not been for a piece of wood obstructing my knees and thwarting my attempt at complete obscurity behind a stack of files and books. My wig provided little cover. Her Honour's keen eye recognised me in a fraction of the time it took for me to recognise her, her mirthless smile cutting like a cold blade to my soul. Life from that point on was about to get significantly more unpleasant.

My wise orations were, almost without exception, gunned down, interrupted and appended with endless pithy references to not having a 'magic wand' or a 'book of spells', apparently the only tools able to 'decipher' my 'unintelligible and 'devoid of substance' legal arguments.

It was with some relief, then, that a brief hiatus in my excoriation manifested at the point when my opponent was berated for not providing an answer to something that no rational person could reasonably be expected to have the answer to. Discomposed and embittered, he sat down, defeated, turned to me and with reference to the judge attempted to whisper the words, 'What a complete fucker!'

What my learned friend had failed to appreciate was the ability of the courtroom microphones to amplify the formerly undetectable, to a universally audible magnitude. To make a bad situation worse, the word 'fucker!' also seemed particularly disposed to amplification.

Now, had there been a tin hat available, I would have worn it, but in its absence I adopted my now familiar position in the trenches, crammed under the bench with my head just poking up from the files, and braced.

What really impressed me was my learned friend's ability to secrete, not only his entire torso under the bench, but his head too, achieving what I had concluded, through my own efforts, was impossible. I suppose if there was ever a time to pull off a Houdini-style disappearing act, it was then, necessity being the mother of invention and all that.

It was one thing being dismissive of Grotbag's observation that one's appearance was redolent of a pig's breakfast, but comparing Her Honour to a squalid fornicator? I bid him farewell.

## Stable Relationship

When the going gets tough, as it had done for my learned friend and me in Court 1, it is always comforting to know that someone has had a worse day than you. That accolade belonged to Mr J. His sentencing hearing was billed as the headline act of the week and, as such, the public gallery was packed to the gunwales with members of the bar who had come to watch. This meant that there was no room for any actual members of the public.

To summarise the facts as briefly as I can, Mr J had been caught midway through an act of love-making with a pony. It was a palomino, so not unattractive, nevertheless the authorities still thought it was wrong!

I understood that there was no denying it. Mr J was observed deep in Treacle's box − literally, not as a turn of phrase − trousers around his ankles, and perched on top of a small stepladder. He had decided, wisely, not to trouble a jury with details of the ungentlemanly act; instead, he had pleaded guilty. The judge now had to decide the appropriate disposal. In that exercise he was assisted by the eloquent submissions in mitigation pleaded by a fresh-faced, and stage-shy, barrister. Rambling as is usual in such exercises, she observed,

'Mr J has completely turned his life around. He has found himself a good job, has qualifications, and is an excellent father to his children.'

She continued,

'Mr J has got himself a new partner and is now happily in a stable relationship.

She didn't even know what she had said. Bellows of laughter that erupted around the courtroom, including guffaws from His Honour the judge no less, lifted the roof, much to her excruciating embarrassment. As much as she may have hoped for the return of courtroom sobriety, the hilarity continued for some time, the only surprise being that nobody called from the public gallery, 'What's her name? Seabiscuit?'

Cases like that of Mr J are not altogether infrequent. Bestiality and other curious sexual behaviours trouble the courts more frequently than you might care to imagine. The lonely sheep farmer herding a member of his flock to a cliff edge before placing hind legs into wellington boots is probably less myth than it is reality. I am sure someone has been convicted of that somewhere. In fact, it is probably bread-and-butter work for the solicitors in Abergavenny. Such cases are also dealt with severely by judges. In passing a sentence of immediate imprisonment on a gentleman who had been convicted of copulating with a Gordon Setter, a notorious northern judge once remarked,

'The grateful dogs of this city can once again walk these streets with ease of mind now that you are behind bars!'

## Kinder Suprise

The main event for this trip was my prosecution of the trial of Mr G. Yes, you heard right, I did say prosecution. The Crown Prosecution Service had realised that I could be as unpleasant to defendants as I could to prosecution witnesses, if paid. In a classic poacher-turned-gamekeeper scenario I was by now prosecuting as much as I was defending: efficiently dispatching those accused of mischief into residences courtesy of Her Majesty's pleasure.

A sort of sixth sense, Mr G explained to the jury, was what had led him to a spot in the park where a voice had told him to start digging. In doing so, he discovered, hidden under a foot of soil, a plastic container from a Kinder Surprise chocolate egg containing some eighteen individual wraps of crack and fourteen of heroin. Understanding, as he did, the scourge of Class-A drugs in society – knowledge gained from his previous career as a drug dealer and his imprisonment as a result of his career – he embraced a sense of public duty, resolved to retrieve the egg, place it in his car and surrender it to the nearest bobby. He was accosted by the police before he had had the opportunity to do so.

As for the few thousand pounds in cash found on his person and in his car that the cynics among us might have assumed represented the proceeds of a drug-dealing enterprise, they could easily be explained, he said, as could the innumerable paper slips evidencing regular cash receipts from gaming machines. My suggestion that Mr G had been feeding drug money into gaming machines and then immediately retrieving it, a common ploy to launder the proceeds of drug-dealing, was dismissed as fantasy. On the contrary, the receipts represented daily wins from the machines to the sum of hundreds of pounds. Those persons who have lost the shirts from their backs as a result of the 'never lose' design of gaming machines simply didn't know the 'magic number'. There is a single magic number which never loses, he told the jury, hence the throughflow of cash. What is that number? Well, that is a tightly held secret, he said. If anyone else knew the number, it would stop working.

What the defendant had not appreciated prior to proffering this ludicrous story for the first time at the police station was the attendance of undercover police officers at the scene who had watched his car from the time he got in until the time he was stopped. They, too, had come to the trial and told the jury that at no point had the defendant left his car at any time, neither had he dug a hole in a park somewhere. The crack and heroin, they explained, can only have been in his possession from the word go, not from a chance discovery beneath some earth.

The jury took two days to deliberate, grappling over an apparent near-impossible decision as to whether the possession of drugs was the product of commerciality, or merely that of enigmatic divination as the defence had contended. By virtue of their eventual, partial, verdict of guilt, the jury must have reluctantly concluded that, whilst it could be that twelve coppers were lying and a mystical treasure map or the like had innocently led Mr G to the drugs in a hole, that probably didn't happen.

As far as the count of money-laundering was concerned, that was a different matter. A secret and magic number which translated into cash and gaming-machine receipts? That was entirely plausible! A robust pronouncement of 'not guilty' on that one was delivered by the foreman, appended by a look in my direction of utter contempt and disgust, cast as if to say, 'How dare you suggest this poor man was anything other than an honest individual with nothing more than the occasional bit of good fortune on his side. Wanker!'

A wise Queen's Counsel once passed to me some sage advice which has ever since formed a guiding principle, 'Never underestimate the stupidity of a jury.'

When I get cases like this, though, I struggle to understand how I could subscribe to such nastiness about the collective acumen of the general public, much less, accuse those sat in the jury box of having an IQ of somewhere between that of a tepid mug of Bovril and a block of lard.

## Oh, How the Other Half Live

My usual form of travel around London was by tube. This was partly to avoid congested roads, but more importantly to allow for urgent case preparation on the way to court. Other times I would travel by road in the love of my life, a beaten-up old builder's van that had been given to me as a thank-you for the restoration of someone's liberty. It had become an essential tool, not only for the transportation of myself and various old motorcycles, but also of residence in times of my frequent impecuniousness and evictions from the crib of a disgruntled love interest.

Legal aid, which accounts for the majority of a criminal barrister's earnings, does not pay well. To earn a fair living, a criminal barrister needs to be efficient, savvy and lucky, as do his clerks. Much of my career in London was managed, it transpired, by clerks who were grossly inefficient, useless and dishonest in equal measure. Chambers was chaos: nobody knew what money was coming in, what was going out, or what anyone was owed. That is, of course, excepting the senior clerk who knew very well how much money had come into chambers because he spent it all in Thailand, leaving the rest of us without even a stick to poke a poo with. Some turned to booze, some lost their wives. For me, my learned advocacy in the Old Bailey of a morning belied my opulent residences: a former dog's bed in the back of a Peugeot Partner van, if not the occasional shelter that accompanied an internet date.

The one shining light came in the form of Amoy's Jamaican Café in Peckham, south-east London, the venue for the bulk of my evening dining and a welcome break from the Tesco pasta pot with tomato and chargrilled chicken that would otherwise be had in the back of the van.

The place was as ramshackle as could be imagined, but I loved it dearly. Among the vinyl-topped tables, bottles of chilli sauce and the odd fake plant, there was always some trouble happening, whether a brawl, a robbery or the peddling of fake £5 notes for a quid a go, advertised on the basis that we all needed a bit of 'Christmas money'. The aromas of Caribbean food that pervaded the place were other-worldly, crafted by the late Charlie, an old boy who hung out in the back among the gigantic pots and pans. He loved to have a chat of an evening but spoke only patois which, for me, was perfectly indecipherable, making for some awkward exchanges. Stews, jerk chicken and goat curry adorned the glass fridges which doubled as the counter and different cakes that 'mum' had crafted were presented on the top, wrapped in cellophane complete with a neon cardboard star advertising the price.

I am not saying that Peckham was rough, but the van would be parked under the CCTV cameras of the local nick in the hope of an outside chance it would still have its wheels and not be on fire by the time I returned. To the all too familiar soundtrack of police sirens, gun-shots, and violence that represented the nocturnal activity of the place, from my chosen parking place I would leg it to this little oasis amongst the tower blocks.

Initially, they wouldn't let me in, fearing that I was some sort of undercover copper. When finally persuaded that I was precisely the opposite, I was welcomed. Out of sympathy for my apparent vagrancy and in return for my repeat custom, the sturdy Jamaican 'momma' took me under her wing, dishing out huge portions of rice and peas and jerk chicken for which I paid next to nothing. Sitting at my usual table in the corner by the window, well away from all of the trouble, some of my finest jury speeches were born.

## Get That Off Your Chest

On this particular voyage to the Woolwich crown court, the police had cordoned off the carpark adjacent to Belmarsh prison to carry out spot checks of the vehicles coming in, presumably in an effort to stymie the tide of contraband goods, phones and drugs that were flowing into the prison. I wasn't of a mind to partake, firstly, because I was late for court and this was going to take some time and, secondly, because I was somewhat embarrassed about the vehicle that I was driving.

I turned around and made my way to a carpark on the other side of the main road. Reasoning, probably not unfairly, that my U-turn might be the product of having something to hide, there then followed something of a police chase. The officer, remaining unconvinced by my explanation that my failure to stop owed merely to an omission to check my mirrors, insisted on searching my van from top to bottom on the premise that I was evading reproach. I didn't have time to hide my copy of *Razzle*, or tidy the mountains of clothes, papers, books, oil-soaked rags, half a sandwich, a bucket with a piece of copper pipe in it, and all the other shit that decorated the back of my home. It was unsurprising then that the policeman wouldn't accept that I was a barrister, even on the production of a wig and gown from beneath a two-by-four piece of plywood. Instead, I was 'accompanied' (read frog-marched) from the car park to the courthouse where a successful identification of me was made by other professional court users and, embarrassingly, my client.

Defeated, although not entirely convinced of my innocent motivations, the police officer was still possessed of enough bare-faced effrontery to tax me with two final questions: why was I was driving a 'shitty plumber's van'? And why was there a trainer in the cab with a jar of olives in it? As if I hadn't suffered enough humiliation.

After exchanging the usual formalities, and an apology for the police escort, my client and I began to get down to brass tacks in preparation of the court day and his trial for assault and dangerous driving.

He had, by this stage of the proceedings, given the police, and indeed his legal team, an unlikely story about how he had had little choice but to pursue and ram his now ex-girlfriend off the road at high speed. He wouldn't plead guilty, instead maintaining that she was 'crazy', that all five foot of her diminutive stature was the personification of violent evil, the progression of which he had been compelled to arrest lest all manner of destructive acts be brought down upon him.

On one of the far distant channels on Freeview, there is a programme called *Boob Station*. It is, in essence, wank-TV, where sad, pathetic and lonely individuals, sock-sheathed ding-a-ling in one hand, credit card in the other, phone up and pay for titillation. There is always an implied promise of an appearance of the panty hamster but, like the carrot on a stick, it never materialises (or gets eaten). Instead the 'models' jiggle their artificially augmented breasts to the apparent excitement, or dissatisfaction, of their, now lighter in the pocket, punters. It is revolting, and I am amazed that any self-respecting individual watches that stuff.

Having had a brief chat with my client outside court while he smoked a fag, a car screeched to a halt on the service road by the doors. Out of it stepped Tracy, who, to my surprise and delight, just so happened to be one of the best models from Boob Station! I recognised her straight away.

Before I could even grapple with the question of the appropriateness or otherwise of an autograph request, she being the complainant in the trial I was to defend, she strode up to my client and without uttering a word, punched him in the head with such force that he was immediately floored and rendered insensible. In the shock, excitement and urgency of the situation some thoughts raced through my mind, and in the following order:

1. Tracy really does have exceptional breasts.
2. I have now witnessed her violence. That will make me a witness and therefore I will not be able to be his advocate. The trial will have to be adjourned.
3. Because of number 2 above, I am not going to get paid. Bollocks!
4. Does my client need an ambulance?

By the time I had got to thought number 4, my client, still dazed, was hauling himself unsteadily to his feet with the use of a nearby bush. Even more surprising than his resurrection, was the apparent instantaneous overlooking of the violent reception that had welcomed him, contradictory mutual declarations of love coming in abandon.

Such was the rapprochement, that Tracy told the judge that, as love trumps all, 'the heart be still as loving, and the moon be still as bright…' and all that sort of stuff, she would not be testifying. It may be no surprise, being a rather strong-willed individual she wasn't going to change her mind, and, in the absence of any other credible evidence, the prosecution had no choice but to throw in the towel. A formal 'not guilty' verdict was entered on the court record.

The best part of the story was that I got paid for the case now that a trial had been avoided. The sad part of this story is that I suspect the bond between the lovebirds didn't survive into a rosy future. On exiting the court, now beyond reproach of the law, the last view of my client was of him leaning out of the passenger window of a taxi, shouting to his beloved, 'See you later, you fucking mentalist,' topped off with a two-fingered salute. I didn't hang around to witness the fallout; I had had all I could take. A brief bit of cover behind the bike racks and then a hop across the road to my van signalled the end of a satisfactory day.

# Judges: the Weird, the Wonderful and the Downright Horrible

We need judges, obviously, to marshall the trials, to sentence, to rule on legal arguments and to deal with all of the ancillaries. They may be regarded as a necessary evil. Some are lovely, most are bright, many are demonic.

I imagine that only a relatively small proportion of the general public are irascible goblins, so why such a high percentage are found on the bench is one of life's imponderables. Many are completely bonkers or otherwise have fundamental personality flaws. I could name judges so vitriolic that they have made barristers cry. I have seen judges that have made prospective jurors cry! For some, their mere presence in court strikes fear into the very soul of all who encounter them.

I surmise that it is for the same reasons that barristers have a disproportionately high degree of turmoil in their home lives and doubtful emotional wellbeing that judges appear as they do. You will see few wedding rings on the fingers of the judiciary to hint at a contented home life. Judges are all too often wedded to the law and the relentless pressure that derives from that. Factor in the obligation to referee bitter, highly intellectual fights and daily exposure to the most disturbing characters and stories that society can produce and you have a good recipe for a few personality quirks.

What I didn't realise when I became a barrister is that judicial impartiality between prosecution and defence is the exception, not the rule; implicit even-handedness is the stuff of fantasy. As a defence barrister you learn pretty quickly that you need to be prepared to battle two prosecutors in a trial: both the prosecutor and the judge. As a student you believe that obsequious capitulation to the will of a judge is always the order of the day. Bollocks! If you want to call yourself a barrister then you have to stand up and fight, otherwise you will be doing your client a disservice and may be complicit in a wrongful conviction. I will regularly invite a jury to totally ignore any opinion the judge gives on the facts when making my final address to them.

Sometimes, a judge will take a dislike to a barrister for no apparent reason. Or perhaps that's just me.

Nobody has despised me more than Her Honour Judge B, who had recently been made up to a circuit judge from her practice in commercial law. She had no affinity with or empathy for the criminal classes, their lives or their legal representatives. Furthermore, she was positively hateful to those she perceived as disposed to un-Christian conduct; this included approximately 100 per cent of my clients. A trial with Judge B on the bench, as you might appreciate, was about as jolly as riding into 'the valley of Death' with 'the six hundred'.

I had managed to get up her nose long before the trial of Mr O, but this trial marked the transition from her merely disliking me to having an unadulterated hatred of me.

Mr O was up for assaulting a traffic warden with a pole. Without hinting at my own view as to the reasonableness of punching an officious council employee whose impetus to get out of bed each morning was the prospect of crapping on someone's day, I had considered that a jury might have some sympathy for the accused. The judge, on the other hand, deemed the whole outrage as entirely un-Christian, although apparently less so than the grotesque act of legally representing the accused! Dressing up the non-defence of 'he deserved it' into legally recognised 'self-defence' was, moreover, just the sort of wickedness that she might have come to expect from me, she might have said. I was in for a rough ride.

In spite of the naked hostility, the interruptions, the scoffing, the eyebrows raised to the ceiling, the shakings of the head and questions such as, 'Do you and your client call yourselves Christians?' in front of the jury (I felt it would be unhelpful to mention that my client was a Muslim and that I was a Buddhist-sympathiser of Jewish descent), I was on course for a certain acquittal. A screw-up by the prosecution in the latter stages of the presentation of their case meant that, to avoid jury prejudice, the trial would have to be aborted and started again. The demonstrable, and admitted, fault of the prosecution in causing the whole affair was as inconsequential as a fart in a hurricane. Her Honour was resolute that it would defy all common sense and reason if the collapse of the trial was considered as anything other than entirely my fault – cynically and criminally manufactured to avoid an inevitable conviction. Distressed, as I was, at the barefaced iniquity, my impassioned protest achieved nothing save a later hearing to decide what sort of judicial punishment I deserved. I had no choice, in the end, but to do that which does not come naturally to me: to sit down and shut up.

The retrial proceeded in a similar vein, resulting not in the 'inevitable conviction' presumed by the judge, but in an acquittal. The jury had grown weary of everyone being told that they weren't Christian, and of the judge attempting to impose her influence. They decided to silence her by delivering a timely verdict of 'not guilty'.

It was all right for them. Making V for 'Victory in Europe' signs as they departed the court, they would never have to see Judge B again. My own smug, self-satisfied expression, on the other hand, was much shorter-lived, erased by the ashen-faced judge whose displeasure deflated my morale like a boot on a bag pipe.

Not two weeks later, fate dealt me another foul blow. A multi-defendant, street-violence trial listed with a time estimate of three weeks was to be presided over by Her Excellency Judge B. A desperate and ill-conceived application to recuse the judge on the basis of her palpable dislike of me failed, but did succeed brilliantly in making her palpable dislike of me even more... palpable.

The night before the trial I had been invited to share a drink with my new neighbours. I had not long before battled storms navigating the south and east coasts and the River Thames in a bid to live aboard a decrepit old sailing boat which I had found abandoned on a mudflat in Dorset. It was assumed to be a moderate improvement on the dog's bed in the van but, regardless, I had reasoned that a one-way descent into Davy Jones's locker one tempestuous night somewhere off the coast of Ramsgate might not be the worst solution to my increasingly unsatisfactory personal life. Unable to afford marina fees in the docklands, I tied up amongst a load of hippies in canal boats in south London. My welding skills were exchanged for the hand of friendship and a blind eye to mooring rules and, whilst reluctant, it was in keeping to agree to a quick drink. That quick drink turned into twelve hippies and I huddling around a burning oil drum at 4.30am complete with doobies being passed round and pangs of foreboding deep within the pit of my stomach.

As you may guess, I was not at my fizziest the next morning. My tactical trial strategy in court, in time-hallowed tradition, was to speak as little as possible and keep my head well below the parapet, an approach that had served me admirably in the past. It had also been working pretty well on this occasion, at least it had, until the fourth witness was called.

This witness to the street violence described how a group had gathered, weapons held aloft. At about this time some unicorns with rainbow manes floated down from the curly white clouds, showering stars as they came. One came over and started nuzzling me. The nuzzling turned to a sharp butt, and then another, and then, 'Oouch!'

I woke up with a start. The unicorn horn was in fact my co-defending barrister's elbow jabbing me purposefully in the ribs. As I turned to face her she whispered, 'The judge has lit up like a fucking tomato!'

Whilst there had obviously been some mixing of metaphors, a quick glance towards the judge revealed the accuracy of my colleague's description. The court was silent, Her Honour had inflated like a cane toad and was incandescent. All eyes were upon me.

I wasn't sure for how long I had been slumbering, but the good-hearted co-defending barrister, who altruistically nursed my sagging nervous system back to health with a dose of exuberant coitus that same evening, recounted a snooze for at least five minutes duration complete with snoring, dribbling and quite possibly farting too.

When confronted with the charge that I had been asleep, a swift riposte that I hadn't been sleeping but merely reflecting deeply on the evidence, elicited a most unhelpful burst of laughter from the jury, which did little to oil the wheels of harmony between counsel and the honourable bench.

Having considered that further orations from me at that particular juncture offered little chance of either pleasure or profit, but could well be fraught with peril, I resigned myself instead to meek subservience, simply accepting both barrels as Her Honour set a new bar in judicial invective. Resisting at the last minute the urge to tell me to stand in the corridor and face the wall for an hour, she did the legal equivalent, which was to write a rambling, six-page letter of complaint to my Head of chambers.

Attending chambers with some trepidation for a meeting with the head to discuss Judge B's letter, I was relieved to encounter him in his usual state of lunchtime inebriation.

'It is a shame that Her Honour Judge B doesn't know me,' he burped, 'because if she did, in the knowledge that I couldn't give a fuck, she wouldn't have bothered'.

A 'good man' and a couple of wholesome slaps on the back restored business to normal. The greatest mercy was that Her Honour Judge B was soon thereafter moved up north. Even today, I still feel pity for the lawyers of Bolton and all others who appear before her. As keen as I once was to visit Greater Manchester one day, I had no choice but to draw a line at Birmingham as being the furthest north I would venture. Even eighty miles away felt a little too close for comfort.

Although this sort of experience is not exceptional, being peculiarly hateful towards a particular barrister wasn't the norm for most judges. They tended to be universally irascible. His Honour Judge D was one such notorious individual. He sat at the inner London Crown Court, an old-fashioned court with rows of benches with ink wells and oak-panelled walls. The barristers gathered in the well of the court, the dock was on a higher terrace at the back, and the judge higher still at the front, cocooned within an oak-clad box. He sat in a tall-backed chair under a single, domed lamp, which swung from the ceiling like a hangman's noose, allowing just enough light to accentuate his sunken cheeks and skeletal features while leaving the rest of us in his ghostly shadow. He was so much part of the furniture, and fitted in so well to the milieu of that room, that we all assumed he had been sat there since the eighteen-hundreds. His manifest resentment of everybody, and everything, was widely assumed to have had its origins in the abolition of the 'black cap' and his authority to utter the words, 'Thou shalt return to the place whence thou camest and hang by the neck till the body be dead.' Sharp as a knife, and more deadly, he would cause all barristers to go weak in the bowels when appearing before him.

Then there was the 'Mad Man'. If your week had gone all right so far, you could remedy that by having a hearing at the Woolwich Crown Court before the 'Mad Man'. He probably needs little more by way of introduction. Most judges were afforded ironic or jovial names by counsel as an affectionate testimonial to their traits, such as 'Mr Happy' or 'Old Gobble Bollocks'. Affection didn't come into it when it came to the 'Mad Man', although I suppose out of respect to the learned judiciary, the prefix 'fucking' was dropped from his title – occasionally. Having the 'Mad Man' as a judge and a bad day were synonymous.

Whilst each court complex invariably housed at least one fearsome judge, Snaresbrook Crown Court had more than its fair share. Judge Q was known for his mordant exchanges with counsel. Regarded fondly as 'stings', they would come in rapid succession, usually appended by chair-tipping recoils of indignation and grimaces worthy of the trophy at a gurning contest. Judge K was simply terrifying, and although you might struggle to see Judge R, a diminutive, nicotine-stained gentleman, you certainly felt his severe tongue-lashings.

While all the aforementioned individuals possessed over-whelming personalities, they were at least able to grab cases and the law by the scruff of the neck. I recall a case when I defended a woman before His Honour Judge R. She had been accused of beating her grandad close to death with a baseball bat. There was no possibility of claiming self-defence as grandpa had been sitting in his armchair reading the paper at the time, but that was the title we gave to the defence in the absence of an actual defence that would fit. The defendant admitted that she had beaten her grandfather, but said that she had done so because he had raped her, repeatedly, for years, as a child and that he deserved everything he had got. That was certainly my view, and probably that of every other right-thinking individual. She had an exceptionally good chance of getting off, the absence of an actual defence being something of an irrelevance.

All of the awful details of those sexual attacks were recounted at my insistence and, having initially tried to stop me through an objection as to relevance, the judge conceded that my arguments were valid, but declared that he had heard enough. Withdrawing a case from a jury in such circumstances usurps the jurors' function and is not generally within the remit of a judge, but a little law and procedure weren't to stand in the way of Judge R and his administration of justice. It was a brave act of mercy, also pragmatism, the likes of which are seldom seen from fresh-faced modern judges.

I was less concerned about those judges with unsettling eccentricities who would nevertheless preside over cases in a fair way, or at least something approaching fairness. The worrying ones are those who will put their egos and addiction to power (colloquially known as 'judgeitis') before fairness.

## 'How Many Years Call Are You?'

Very occasionally, one encounters a judge who simply isn't fit for purpose. The reputation of Judge T preceded him. He was obnoxious, patronising, pompous, not to mention useless, obtuse, prejudiced and unfair, and those were just his best qualities. He would habitually attack counsel for no reason at all. Some were hurt and upset by it, others, like me, couldn't give a toss.

When making a very carefully constructed legal argument one day, he interrupted me and, in an attempt to be condescending, said, 'How many years call are you?'

This means, how long had I been doing the job? I think my youthful good looks had deceived him a trifle because he looked rather taken aback when I said fifteen years.

'Oh, er, oh, er…,' he blustered. 'You see Mr N over there? He is thirty years' call,' as if to say that he was a proper barrister in contrast to the young upstart that currently appeared before him.

'Why don't you just fuck off?' is an enquiry that I could well have made of him, had my wiser head not prevailed.

## Thanks for the Lesson

I had become embroiled in a legal argument with a learned recorder who looked about nineteen years old. He was also lacking in skills of legal analysis, but nevertheless thought it fit to reward my recalcitrance with an *auditoribus educationem*. With his 'Noddy's Guide to Criminal Law' in hand he asked of me sententiously:

'Would you like to sit whilst I educate you on the law?'

'I prefer to be nourished whilst standing,' I replied.

'Oh, and why don't you just piss off, you insufferable little twat?' is something that could well have been said, had I not considered it a little injudicious.

## Pissing on the Chips

To the disgruntled defendant who discreetly urinated on the judges' lunches, resulting in the immediate closure of the Snaresbrook Crown Court catering facilities, not to mention a reputed 'fire-breather style' eruption of partially chewed potato against the wall, shame on you! That is vigilantism and you get no sympathy from us. Well, maybe a bit.

## Carousel Catastrophe

The poker face is one of counsel's most essential tools.

It took me years to perfect and was hard-earned. Being able to look a jury in the eye and tell them with a straight face that it is entirely credible that your client was a good Samaritan, returning televisions through a broken shop window at 3am and not, as charged, stealing them, as I once did, takes immense skill. Being able to maintain a poker face when the resident judge at Snaresbrook falls off his chair is a skill that I clearly don't possess.

As His Honour Judge L leant forward to retrieve a file from a tiered carousel holding about thirty, the front casters on his large, leather chair accelerated in reverse beneath him. A desperate attempt to prevent the inevitable by grasping the carousel, alongside cries of, 'Heavens!', 'Good Lord!' and 'Crikey, Moses!', succeeded only in sending the carousel crashing to the floor with a noise reminiscent of an attack on a hoarder's saucepan collection. Like a condemned prisoner on the gallows, His Honour's figure dropped from view and the courtroom fell silent, save for the delayed comedy cymbal crash from a loose carousel tier as it wobbled away and lost its fight with the courtroom door.

I remain impressed to this day by the deftness shown by the other barristers in keeping a straight face, moreover, harbouring expressions of sincere concern as they enquired as to His Honour's welfare. It made my uncontrollable convulsions seem all the more inappropriate and, as we all know, laughter being inappropriate does little to quell the splitting of one's sides. Pretending that I was picking up a pen from the floor, I remained doubled over trying not to piss my pants, praying at the same time that I would not be called upon to speak. A co-defendant had forgotten to switch off his phone and, mercifully, it rang at the opportune moment, the ring tone being the theme tune from the film 'The Great Escape'. Quite fitting in the circumstances, I thought. It brought to pass an extremely welcome coffee break.

## Hot Dog Roll or Cocktail Stick

I have met all sorts of people over the years during my early morning swim at the Atherton Leisure Centre in East London. His Honour Judge B, naked in the showers, was one image that I was not expecting to confront. He had already seen me strolling in, thus making a hasty retreat impossible. I had no choice but to discuss the finer legal intricacies of R v Smith as the learned judge lathered his swinging undercarriage with lashings of Imperial Leather. Always on the lookout for opportunities, I pondered whether I should congratulate His Honour on his well-proportioned genitalia in the hope of banking some house points. I reasoned, however, that his west-facing weenie, gallant as it was, looked a little feeble in comparison to my southern-hanging, and altogether more generous, Mr Happy. He would think I was taking the piss. Besides, he had endured years of my courtroom bullshit and didn't need any more.

# The Old Bailey

There are few institutions more famous than the Old Bailey, occupying the site of the former Newgate Prison in the heart of the City of London. It is the court that gets to try the really grizzly stuff. In keeping with the ambience of the place, down in the bowels of the court there remain the remnants of the 'dead man's walk', a series of ever-decreasing arches leading from the condemned prisoner's cell to the gallows, designed that way so as to prevent the condemned from attempting an escape as the hand of the Grim Reaper stretched out to greet them. The quiet, echoing corridors and atriums that service the large, imposing courtrooms house glass displays containing articles associated with the administration of justice in years gone by. They are all reminders of the might of the judicial system and add to the imposing nature of the institution. I find the atmosphere to be strangely eerie and wonder whether the bricks and mortar have literally absorbed the horrors and sadness that have echoed down the years through the chambers.

A climb up the marble spiral staircase will reward you with a view of the London skyline and of the golden statue of Lady Justice standing proudly on top of the dome above Court Number One, symbolising impartiality and justice. Famous trials in the court have included those of Oscar Wilde, the Krays, Doctor Crippin, the Yorkshire Ripper and Ruth Ellis, the last woman to be executed in the UK, to name but a few.

There are a number of traditions peculiar to the Old Bailey. The judges have to be addressed as 'My Lord' or 'My Lady', as opposed to 'His Honour', or 'Her Honour', and junior counsel are not permitted to use lecterns to rest their papers. Lecterns are for Queen's Counsel only, who also enjoy their own exclusive dressing and dining facilities. As in the Court of Appeal, not a stone's throw away, the judges of the Old Bailey are often sharper and more experienced than your average judge. Certainly, when finding one's feet as an advocate, the whole environment can feel quite intimidating, as well as very exciting. That extra stimulation inherent in appearing at a venue so steeped in history and legend lends a feeling almost of ethereal surrogacy for the eminent legal talents that have appeared there over years gone by. Maybe the spirit of the place has been the reason for it being home to some of my most flamboyant and memorable successes.

Although Old Bailey judges are generally occupied with cases of the utmost seriousness, at the end of the day, the Old Bailey is but a crown court like any other. If there aren't many murders knocking around, the Bailey will help out other crown courts with work. I have, of course, experienced the pressure of defending 'death' at the Bailey, and successfully I might add, but if I am honest, my appearances were more usually associated with what we affectionately call in the trade, 'the shite'. I was more familiar with the embarrassment associated with opening a case to an expectant jury, explaining that they wouldn't be troubled with body parts or scenes of gruesome homicides this time, but would instead be grappling earnestly with the dishonest removal of two packets of razors, three packets of Durex and £7 worth of meat from Tesco, than I was with the emotions consistent with being the spokesman for a murderer.

The downside of a defendant appearing before a seasoned Old Bailey judge is that the judge is unaccustomed to handing down anything other than a life sentence. Ten years to a judge of the Central Criminal Court is akin to a Jaffa cake and a cup of tea.

I once prosecuted a lad in his early twenties for dealing a few tablets of ecstasy at a music festival. He hadn't been in trouble before and was much like a rabbit in the headlights when he took to the witness box. Throughout the trial the judge mocked him and joked, saying things like, 'Was that pocket money from your mum?' and, 'Do your parents know you are here?' It seemed hard for His Lordship to take seriously something which was comparatively trivial compared with his daily grind. I gave the defendant a really hard time, too, and then felt bad when he was convicted, as I sometimes do when prosecuting. I felt somewhat better when the judge told him that he would take mercy on him this time and would give him another chance by passing a light sentence.

As he pronounced the six-year term of immediate incarceration, the knees went and emotional breakdown followed, and that was just me. The poor lad fainted in the dock and had to be carried away by the jailors.

## Famous at Last

Film crews are an almost daily appearance at the Old Bailey, reporting all the hideous details of courtroom testimony. I was lucky enough to appear on a news broadcast on my debut there. As Queen's Counsel discussed the day's events in a notorious murder trial with the BBC, I was contemporaneously battling the effects of a stiff breeze on my Iceland carrier bag containing my case papers. I think it was at about the time that Queen's Counsel expressed deep regret that the body of the deceased mother of two had never been discovered that my bag, adorned with the logo 'Mum's gone to Iceland', flew past the camera with me in hot pursuit, to the bewilderment of all. On the *News at Ten* you could just about see me in the corner of the frame, jumping on the Iceland bag with both feet before punching the air victoriously.

## Empty Your Pockets

All crown courts have significant security at their front doors, including X-ray machines and metal detectors.

This is perfectly understandable as those inclined to carry weapons and act violently are the types of characters who frequent crown courts. The Old Bailey is the hottest of the lot on security. To get in, you are required to submit to all sorts of searches and detectors before passing through a type of air lock. It might stop the place being stormed by armed attackers, but it also creates a hell of a queue at the doors. This was the situation when I attended for the fourth day of a rape trial I was defending.

There were tuts and sighs from behind me as I set off the metal detector for a third time, prompting an urgent, final search. Feeling some tinfoil in my back left suit pocket, I realised that that must be the culprit and without looking at it, tossed it nonchalantly towards the bowl on the table. It was still in the air when I was struck by the stomach-turning realisation that I had just frisbeed a prophylactic across the packed reception area of the Old Bailey. Some laughed, others turned away in disgust, and precisely nobody bought my protestations that the offending article was merely an exhibit in the case. If anything, the implausibility of that suggestion just seemed to evoke even more hilarity. Vain attempts to hush the incident were thwarted courtesy of the apparent 'pervert beacon' conspicuously located on top of the metal detector which, excruciatingly, continued to beep and flash unabated. It lacked only a neon arrow pointing in my direction inscribed with the word 'pest' to enhance the effect.

I promise that I hadn't brought the apparatus as some sort of sordid adornment to an anticipated career demonstration by the handcuff-proficient, and notably good-looking jailor in the cells below. It's true that, generously, a night or so previously, she had participated in justice-furthering experiments necessary for me to confidently contradict the complainant in the case, but today it was purely for demonstration purposes only. The main witness in the trial had claimed that the defendant had used a single hand both to unwrap a condom and put it on: an accomplishment which in my view was unlikely. (I wasn't going to invite the jury to consider teeth, a method demonstrated by my obliging understudy.) I considered it judicious to persuade the jury of my findings with the help of a little practical display.

The police officer in the case glowed with embarrassment as she was handed the thing along with a request that she open it with a single hand. Judicial asperity erupted at the prospect of yet more 'unpalatable theatrics' and the jury was sent out to save their ears from His Lordship's forthcoming 'kindly advice', but not before the police officer had failed in the task she had been set.

Every victory has a price, and I was never going to leave there entirely unscathed or without some not insignificant 'judicial guidance'. But, when all was said and done, it wasn't just a carrier bag full of papers, an old apple core and my tail between my legs that I left with. I also clutched the back of a fag packet with the words 'Not Guilty' written on it, and an emphatically unopened condom.

## I Will Cut You From Here to Here

It isn't only the judges who are potent at the Old Bailey; so, too, are the old salts who frequent the place, kicking up dust in the arena.

Over a period of a month or so, I found myself defending a lorry driver who had driven the biggest haul of amphetamines the UK had ever seen from Holland to London. The drugs had been hidden in flowerpots which had been collected from Germany.

The prosecution alleged that in seeking to hide his detour from Germany to Holland, the defendant had 'cooked up' the tachograph in his lorry, the manipulation having been very carefully done. Tachograph interpretation is extremely complex and an area of expertise in itself. It took me a week to get my head around it, and a day-long speech to explain it to the jury.

There were two other co-defendants in the case, both of whom had been caught unloading the amphetamines on their arrival in London. The defence of all three was that they were ignorant of the nature of the items they were handling, believing they were flowerpots, and nothing more.

My case had gone brilliantly, until the presentation of the case for the second defendant identified a bump in the road that I had failed, hitherto, to appreciate. When in London, the two other co-defendants were observed by undercover police officers to go straight to the boxes of amphetamines which were secreted in the very centre of the lorry. All of the boxes, whether they contained plant pots or amphetamines, were identical. Why then would they start unloading from the centre of the lorry if they were ignorant as to the contents of the boxes located there?

My client's case was that the amphetamines must have been loaded in Germany at the plant-pot factory and not, as suggested, in Holland, where plant pots were displaced for amphetamines. He denied having knowledge of any differences between the boxes; he just stood back as they were loaded. The co-defendants' case, as it transpired, was that they had been directed to unload the boxes in the centre by the lorry driver, aka my client!

There is a legal expression for an invidious set of circumstances such as these: a 'fucking disaster'.

Conflict between defendants, which at worst can develop into a full-on 'cut-throat' situation is never what you want. Defendants pointing fingers at each other generally leads to counsel for the defence doing the work for the prosecution and all the defendants being found guilty. There was no obvious easy way out of this one other than to suggest to the second defendant in the witness box that he was lying and had had prior knowledge, and not from the lorry driver, that the boxes in the centre of the lorry were the ones of interest to him. Some might argue that that would tend to undermine his case; others, that it would tear the entire arse out of it.

You may not be surprised to learn that I wasn't exactly bursting with the joys of spring when I caught up with the second defendant's counsel in the foyer at lunch time. He was a Queen's Counsel, a delightful old boy who had been knocking about the Bailey since the dawn of the age. He had been warm, avuncular and jovial during the trial so far, not unlike the benevolent grandad who would dip into his wallet and give you a quid every time you visited him as a child. It pained me to tell him of my predicament, and that there seemed no way out but to confront his client with the conflict of accounts.

He smiled warmly and laid a comforting hand on my shoulder. As his friendly blue eyes met mine, he whispered,

'If you do that, I will cut you from here to here.'

As he did so, he ran a finger slowly across his throat and then down to his navel before bidding me a good afternoon and making his way to the lunch room for QCs.

I remain unconvinced even to this day that his simulated disembowelment was a metaphorical forecast only. I was sufficiently chilled to steer clear of further enquiry. It may suffice to say that I found another way around the problem, albeit one that failed to avoid a ten-year holiday for my client, courtesy of the Queen.

## Inflammatory Language

Youth on my side, the weight of the world on my shoulders and bubbling over with a whole raft of gripes with nobody to whinge to, I sat my old man down one day and vented. I told him of my latest case in which, in passing sentence and a harsh one at that, the judge had gravely offended both my client and me by remarking that my client's assault on her dear late grandmother had been a 'frenzied attack'. I was incensed at the audacious exaggeration and asked my dad whether I should say something about it.

'What were the facts?' my dad asked.

'Well, she stabbed her granny ninety times with a kitchen knife, believing that she was the devil, and then burnt the house down' came my reply.

My dad's posture slumped, 'Might be time for a different day job, son!'

# The Court of Appeal

I struggle to think of any place that has proved quite as adept as the Court of Appeal in engendering such profound fear within me, apart from maybe the public conveniences on the A40 to Oxford which I visited one evening wearing a pair of jodhpurs. It is the one place where none of us wants to go.

If there has been some screw-up in the case somewhere along the line, the manifestation of which may call into question the safety of a conviction or the appropriateness of a sentence, then you owe it to your client to put pen to paper and write to the appeal judges. If they think you might have a point, you are invited to the Royal Courts of Justice on The Strand in London to make your peace with a selection of the most acute legal minds in the country. Without exception, the bench of judges, usually three, comprises revered and redoubtable characters.

Like the Old Bailey, the place is steeped in history. Walking through the oak-panelled doors of the expansive

Victorian Gothic-style building, you are immediately exposed to the musty aroma of history, represented, as in the old Bailey, by corridors of glass cabinets containing legal artefacts of a bygone era. Beyond the metal detectors at the doors, you must hurry through the echoing cathedral-like Great Hall before negotiating labyrinthine corridors, cloisters, marble galleries and wrought-iron gateways which, with a fair wind, will lead you to the advocates' robing room. With a short hiatus for a nervous pee-stop in the bogs followed by a sharp climb up some stone steps, you find yourself at your destination: one of a row of old, oak-panelled courtrooms, adorned with wrought-iron bookshelves that house dusty, old law books from floor to ceiling. There you await your fate.

You will see barristers from all over the country, but seldom a familiar face. There is little conversation between counsel; all are desperately reading, cramming, swotting in the hope of having a fair chance of answering the questions that will shortly be flung at them. The one thing that all the barristers have in common is the possession of dirty underwear. Let me be frank with you. As barristers we are all quacks and charlatans. We essentially dress up in mummy's clothes, don a stilted manner of speech, throw in a bit of Latin here and there and wing it. Ninety-nine percent of the time, this cavalier approach works out fine, but not one of us truly knows what the bloody hell we are doing. The Court of Appeal is different. You are expected to know your onions. You are also expected to be conversant with the law, God forbid. We all drop the ball sometimes but if ever there is going to be a high chance of it happening, and catastrophically, it will be here.

After robing up, but before being granted access to the courtroom, all of the barristers line up on the wooden benches outside. Just as when awaiting the first appointment with the boss following accidentally 'ccing' him into the email where you called him a 'useless bloater', spirits are subdued and the atmosphere is thick with foreboding. The only sound comes from the occasional rustling of paper or the gentle mopping of a bead of sweat from a brow.

If you are incredibly lucky, the judges won't want to hear from you, having been sufficiently uninspired by your written advice and grounds of appeal to be undesirous of their cerebellums being further dulled by oral submissions. Usually, they *will* want to hear from you. Usually, they are a bit bored and will want to play with you, like a cat plays with a frog, beginning with decapitation and ending with generous distribution of the entrails.

Unlike other courts, where advocacy usually adopts a form not dramatically different from that of polite conversation, here it is more akin to delivering a soliloquy from the moment the curtains part. Advocacy like this is unusual and nerve-wracking, made worse when your audience is brighter and better read than you are. They expect you to tell them what you want them to do and why. You can expect to be interrupted frequently and confronted with taxing questions. Beware those who haven't done their homework. Failure to provide a cogent answer results swiftly in derision, chastening and public humiliation, all of which are played out before the other punters who, heads bowed, nervously await their turn to strut and fret their time upon the scaffold.

Although at the time of my re-establishment in the Midlands I had a proper bed in a rented property, the overnight stay before the hearing would nevertheless always remain the province of the van. I would park up at the hippy camp in south London where my, by now, increasingly derelict boat still lay. On a couple of occasions my friend W, more on whom later, would find himself at the Court of Appeal at the same time as me. He would join me in the back of the van, sleeping top to tail on the dog's bed. In the morning, the side door would slide open and we would come bounding out like Hannibal and Faceman from *The A-Team*. Granted, it would have been more authentic had we also fashioned some high explosives out of a bog roll and blown up the county jail, but instead we made do with an energetic leap over the puddle of pee representing the night's incidences of relief and prepared for the day ahead. Throwing on our suits within view of the surrounding flats, we then rushed off to The Strand and won our appeals.

What I found curious about my experiences there is how, against all the odds, my performances would, at least intermittently, be considered competent. I would occasionally have a kind of out-of-body experience – I think the shrinks call it 'depersonalisation' – when I could hear somebody talking a degree of sense, but would scarcely believe it was me. I would simultaneously be pre-occupied with the inner voice reminding me that I was still a simpleton who habitually peed in the sink without having the courtesy to remove the pots and pans first, and what the hell did I think I was doing standing here? Quite distracting, in fact.

## Vigorous Commuting on the Last Train to Lewisham

Privately-funded cases are few and far between, so when you do get hold of one, you tend to want to hang on to it.

Mr B had been caught allegedly engaging in sordid acts of self-abuse while riding the last 'night train' back home from Lewisham. He had come to see me on the basis that I had a formidable reputation for such matters (by which I mean defending the innocent, not partaking).

My first job was to gently break the news to him that my modest professional fees would make the subject matter of his indictment quite possibly the most expensive wank in history, dwarfing the usual expenditure associated with his proclivities: the odd sheet of Kleenex, sock or even prophylactic if he was feeling 'posh'. What price, though, do you put on freedom of expression? Oh, and, er, liberty. After coughing up his hard-earned cash into the sweaty palm of my clerk, he was diverted away from the chaotic engine room behind the scenes and into the salubrious façade that was our conference room. Cup of tea in hand, Mr B regaled me with his account of the evening's events.

It was true, said Mr B, that he was a little worse for booze, but he was nevertheless possessed of his faculties. The train was packed to the rafters and it was by reason of the same jostling that led to his confinement in a small corner of the carriage that the zip on his trousers breathed its last. Whether his trouser-snake had also popped out for a breath of air was a matter of conjecture, but what he could say, categorically, was that the supposed act of self-stimulation was nothing more than a furious, innocent, and indeed honourable, attempt to fix his broken zip.

I have encountered many instances of 'flashing' in my career. One particularly memorable one was that of a gentle-man who had leapt from the bushes in Wolverhampton Park and exposed himself over a banner which read romantically, 'Sonia, will you marry me?!' The prosecution claimed that it had ruined the moment for her intended, diverting her gaze from the eyes of her Romeo to that of a ring-bearer of an altogether more malodorous nature. The action of Mr B, however, was even greater in its alleged intrepidity.

What I do find intriguing are the very different attitudes encountered to this type of offending. While I don't seek to minimise something which can vary in the degree to which it is sinister, and clearly has the capacity to cause people real distress, reactions to it are extremely varied. For example, on one occasion, a young lady making her way from Tesco Express, Surrey Quays to Canada Water train station, frequently lifted her skirt to reveal her lack of underwear and her well-ventilated southern regions.

She was rather like the Pied Piper of Hamlyn, I feared, leading a group of about twenty men, four rows deep, to their possible doom in the mountain.

What was striking about the whole thing was the complete absence of any complaint or anyone who was offended or disgusted. Well, at least until I was displaced from the front row that is!

By way of contrast, the off-duty police officer who had witnessed Mr B's skirmish with his serpent was demonstrably less impressed. I suspect the truth about Mr B was that he had been so drunk as not to be cognisant of his surroundings, believing erroneously that he was in the privacy of his garden shed, inhaling his wife's underwear and not, as he was, bashing one off on the 00.15 to Gravesend. The well-known broken-zip defence, however, was the one we were going to pursue to guaranteed victory. It felt a bit unkind having just been handed a modest sum of cash to tell him that he was, to coin a legal phrase, screwed, and so I didn't. I would let the jury do that.

I had turned down so much alternative work in a bid to litigate this case, not because it was relatively lucrative, but because it was just bloody amusing! The sniggers that had reverberated around the courtroom in the early preparatory hearings where the salient issues of 'vigorous zip-fixing' had been mooted had been indicative of fun times to come. It was a very sad day, then, when the listing of another important trial meant that I had no choice but to give the case of Mr B away to my good old friend Jo.

It was about 8.30 in the morning that I received a text from Jo which began:

'You twat, ...'

There was nothing unfamiliar about that on the face of it, brotherly love and all that, but it continued, 'the judge has ordered us to attend court at 8am today to conduct "trouser experiments".'

He went on to recount how the judicial proposal that the defendant be dressed in the heavily semen-stained court exhibit number one, his trousers, and paraded around the court so it could be observed whether or not his zip would hold fast, was met with some not insignificant opposition from the legal teams. The absence of a bargepole for use by counsel to handle the exhibit had also engendered some consternation. The donning of rubber gloves adequate to comfortably manoeuvre the article so suffused with ejaculate that it was described as extending from 'arsehole to Christmas', had interfered with Jo's fragile temperament, warranting, as he claimed, the outpouring of extraordinarily abrasive language in his text message to me.

Nothing was discerned to be amiss with the zip, so there followed an hour-long legal argument concerning the admissibility of the semen staining. The prosecution averred that the defendant had been witnessed choking his chicken to within an inch of its life on the last train from Lewisham and, lo and behold, as if by magic, a giant semen stain was observed on his crotch. Why then, they queried, were they even having a legal argument about evidence that was so obviously probative?

'On the contrary…', replied Jo. In the eloquent manner for which he was well known, he respectfully observed that his faithful client was a 'prolific wanker', whose predilections were undoubtedly responsible for numerous incidences of soilage. The evidence, he loquaciously submitted, was just as consistent with the notion of previous, and altogether legal, acts of romantic self-flagellation as they were with a railway rampage.

It seems his speech to the jury was one of his finest. Opening with some First World War poetry, he began, 'Members of the jury, the enemy has exposed himself on our left flank.'

He proceeded to aver that it was entirely plausible that rhythmical zip maintenance could be misread as worm-burping, at one point entreating the jury to reject the claims of the querulous female police officer who had witnessed the whole supposed outrage.

'This man must be discharged forthwith!' he exclaimed forthrightly, simultaneously banging the table in a flamboyant display that raised a chorus of laughter from the jury. 'Waste no time in relieving him,' he demanded.

He continued to implore them,

'Cup your hands ladies and gentlemen and receive these most learned ejaculations.'

His accidental/deliberate mistake in referring to the *actus reus* ('guilty act') as the 'actus rearus' would, for most of us, have been the final straw that ensured our professional defenestration, but a deep inhalation from His Honour the judge and his reclining in his chair signalled his resignation to the comedy routine as it unfolded.

The jury knew, as did everyone, that Mr B had been mercilessly beating his own drum that evening, but for a man who had entertained them so thoroughly for a week, and in whose face they had laughed, it was uncharitable to now criminalise him. It was, therefore, to the utter exasperation of the prosecution that Mr B, duly found innocent, walked from the court, his head held high, his shoulders square to the wind and in a pair of securely fastened pantaloons.

## This Man is a Troll

Jo opened to the jury a prosecution of a defendant on trial for malicious communications and harassment offences arising from his online activity. The defendant was also somewhat unfortunate-looking and rather short.

'Members of the jury, the man you see in the dock is a troll,' he announces. Laughter rebounds around the jury box.

# How Can You Represent Somebody You Know is Guilty?

The sole purpose for including my ramblings on this topic is that it is *the* most frequently asked question. Instead of groaning and answering flippantly the next time someone asks, I can simply extort money from them in exchange for a copy of my book. It is also a question that is not straightforward to answer; it calls for reflection and introspection.

On a simple analysis, I am prohibited by the barristers' code of conduct from knowingly advancing the interests of somebody who is offering up a false defence. For example, if I am told by my client that he *had* killed his wife but he was going to tell the jury that he hadn't, then I would be unable to represent him. In the event that he told me that he had killed his wife and was simply seeking my advice as to his options, I would tell him either to plead guilty or, consistent with the burden of proof which lies at the heart of a fair judicial system, consider simply testing the sufficiency of the prosecution case, but without advancing a positive defence.

If the defendant gives me a cock-and-bull story, such scenarios accounting for ninety per cent of my professional time, then I am obliged to articulate his defence before the court. That isn't to say that I wouldn't already have given the defendant firm advice as to my views of his prospects and possibly negotiated with the prosecution potential alternative charges. For the cases where the trial does proceed, and with a defence that the barrister perceives to be nonsense, one argument often made is that 'the truth will out'. If the barrister believes it all to be a cart-load of horse shit, then so will a jury. Justice will prevail; so far so, so virtuous.

Is justice denied, though, when a defence barrister persuades a jury of a case which he or she does not believe? This is where I struggle, particularly as such situations have predominated in my practice. The simple 'get-out' is to say that my views as to guilt or innocence are inconsequential and non-guiding. It is the view of the jury that matters. I could also suggest that if the prosecutor is as able to influence a jury as the defence barrister, then justice will weave a middle path between advocates, with the evidence being the deciding factor. If this analysis is sound, then what we certainly don't want is a more able prosecutor than defender because the scales would be tipped away from favouring the defence, leaving the door open to a wrongful conviction.

I still can't help feeling a little dissatisfied by all this, though. I am a spin doctor, an illusionist, a chancer and philanderer, who has spent his life honing the techniques of persuasion. On a daily basis I conjure images in the minds of laypeople that I don't personally believe bear any relationship to the truth. I study my audience; I seduce them; I play to them. I throw stars in their eyes, and dish up red herrings, sometimes when the hangman's noose casts a grim shadow. Are they young or old? Is that juror a bookworm or a wild child? Are they drawn to the evidence, or do their minds stray to fantasies of a fling with one of the barristers, the question of what to have for tea that evening, or whether it was still raining outside? I adapt my patter accordingly, like the love-child of an octopus and an escapologist, appealing to the preoccupations of the moment, with sabotage of the Crown case as the prize.

It is undoubtedly the case that guilty people continue to get away with things because of me, when otherwise they would not. How do I feel about this? Am I diverting the course of justice, rather than being a fundamental part of it? Am I the cause of injustice, or the cure?

Looking at it on the macro level, if your standard defendant didn't feel that he could find a defence barrister who would fight his corner to the best of his or her ability, then that absence of trust would lead to self-representation which would almost certainly result in miscarriages of justice, not to mention substantial delays to the entire system of justice. Defence barristers being good at what they do is therefore fundamental to the operation of the system. In addition, if my work in court was affected in any way by my suspicions as to the defendant's guilt, then there might be a problem should those suspicions be entirely erroneous.

There are cases, believe it or not, where the defendant is innocent, or at least not guilty of that with which he has been charged, and the ability to thoroughly rip the arse out of the prosecution case and persuade the jury of the same is vital. Those skills are inseparable from those that cause a jury to acquit someone who is guilty, as yin is to yang. Better to have guilty people walking free than innocent people in prison.

I do struggle to be convinced, though, of some of the arguments which attempt to justify the bare fact that I spend a lot of my time restoring the liberty of people who don't deserve it. The better the defence barrister is compared with the prosecutor, the greater the likelihood of undeserving people getting off. It is a curious profession in which peers applaud cunning and deception; barristers who manage to pull off acquittals against the weight of evidence are hailed as true masters of the art. The competitiveness between barristers means that winning a case makes you a winner! It feels good. If you have achieved a seemingly impossible feat then you feel the rush of success. Moreover, if you succeed, you will get more work and, in turn, you might just manage to pay the bills that month. In spite of it all, for me at least, conflicted feelings lie just beneath the surface.

You may recall my folly of the condom in the Old Bailey and the case to which it pertained. I secured an acquittal for that defendant, who, as a subsequent jury found, went on a week later to violently rape a lone woman one night in a park. I was pleased to be chosen to defend that case, too; a consequence of my earlier 'success' on his behalf in court.

But who could fail to reflect on the fact that the opportunity to commit such an appalling crime in the first place was afforded by an earlier acquittal by a jury of which I played a central part?

They say that the flap of a butterfly's wings in Brazil can trigger a tornado in Texas; that every action has knock-on effects resonating into the future that one may not hope for or desire. But whereas the person who lost their house in Texas may harbour no antipathy toward the butterfly, the same may not be said of the victim to the lawyer who deftly returned a predator to the streets. The internal conflicts that defence barristers have to confront may be all too obvious.

Take as another example Mr G, in whose acquittal for the rape of his nephew I had played a leading role, managing to engender enough confusion for the jury as to the alleged location of the attack, whether it occurred on an upper or lower bunk bed, to leave them with little option other than to acquit. Mr G contacted my clerks six months later with the request that I be sent to the court to represent him on a drug charge. When I met him in the cells, he told me that he didn't actually need my representation, but wanted me to stand next to him when he pleaded guilty to the new charge. It would mean that I would be paid well for very little work. This was just his way of saying thank you for the fantastic work that I had done on his behalf before. His case could have been dealt with some time ago, but he was determined to wait in the cells in order to make this gesture. How was I supposed to feel about him? Was he my best friend, the devil incarnate, or both?

When you boil it all down, you are confronted by the inescapable conclusion that you are closer to a professional conman than you might care to admit. My own internal conflicts are at least mollified when I consider the one thing that cannot be denied: our justice system has developed over centuries to be the best and the fairest in the world, one that it is either emulated, or envied by jurisdictions all around the globe. As the fairest possible route to justice, it is probably the best that any society could do.

# Everyone Hates You

'To be an effective criminal defence counsel, an attorney must be prepared to be demanding, outrageous, irreverent, blasphemous, a rogue, a renegade, and a hated, isolated, and lonely person – few love a spokesman for the despised and damned'
Clarence Darrow (1857–1931)

For all the humour, the theatre and the fun, the unique features of the job and the personality traits of those to whom it appeals lend themselves to a recipe for personal affliction. Self-admiration and self-importance is inbred in all barristers. After all, a jury will never believe someone who doesn't believe in him- or herself. Large measures of egoism, albeit tempered by a learned empathy for others, establishes the leadership qualities vital to being the top dog in the courtroom. It is courtesy of a morbid self-belief that the barrister is enabled to swing punches to the bitter end on behalf of some hideous characters, when, at times, the jury hate him, the witnesses hate him, his opponent hates him, the judge hates him, and all the people in the public gallery hate him. Sometimes, even his ungrateful bastard of a client hates him. Yes, it is only a job, and an essential one for the course of justice, but you will still be despised for doing it on more occasions than are healthy.

For me, as I suspect is the case for others, the lure of the profession was always to take centre stage, to be admired and successful. It is the goal of being better than everyone else – faster, sharper, more cunning – that provided the drive, leaving as subsidiary any interest in overseeing the effective administration of justice. When the spotlight is on and the court is hushed in readiness for your closing monologue that might just mean the difference between a life sentence and liberty; it all rests on you. The dizzying cocktail of adrenaline and dopamine intrinsic in the prospect of a win gives a hit like a shot of heroin. The greater the stakes and the higher the odds, the greater the hit. In precisely the same way that gamblers need to search for the next bit of stimulation regardless of the outlay, it is what I lived for.

As is the case for any addict, those who expose themselves to regular, exceptional 'hits', and indeed those who feel the need to constantly test their own worth or strive for perfection, are only ever one step away from a crash. The early days of not-guilty verdicts would give me a high for days. There might follow a mild flattening of the mood eventually, or maybe not if I was already on to the next case, but just as for a crack addict, the effect of each hit over time became less pronounced. The lows, on the other hand, became ever more enhanced. It was by years of denial and unhealthy distractions that the fog, tiptoeing up from behind, had begun to engulf me unimpeded, helped by the constant pressure, the fights and the isolation. It was a mercy that my vices, unlike those of many of my peers, did not include the excessive use of drink or drugs in an attempt to assuage the blues. For some, these spelled oblivion.

The peaks and troughs of the game seemed to tip everyone off an even keel, even in the unlikely event that they were of sound mind at the beginning of their career. Of all of my closest legal friends, I can think of precisely none that didn't struggle to some degree with their mental health or the vicissitudes of life generally.

Jo, the most dazzling advocate I know, verged on mania, such was his ebullience in court. He was a genius. He also enjoyed a good drink. It was Russian roulette whether a telephone call to him would be received in his matrimonial home or from the Holiday Inn Express in Stratford East 15 where, customarily, he would be banished by his good lady wife on account of his 'drunken intransigence' and cynicism. Like me, and so many others in the profession, he had to endure the additional stresses of being constantly broke. At his lowest ebb, he had recently delivered a speech of unmatched brilliance in a notorious kidnap case in which we were co-defending. His inspirational address was delivered as a parody of *Romeo and Juliet*. Glorious as it was, though, he had failed to fully consider the consequences. The jury, who had been captivated by his pastiche of the famous tragedy, enthusiastically participated in the immersive theatre. Regarding my client as representative of the wicked Montagues and his of the Capulets, they promptly convicted both.

Both defendants had been gifted to us by a loyal firm of instructing solicitors and, thanks to the Chuckle Brothers here managing to land each of them a few years of porridge, neither of us ever worked for the solicitors again. It had elevated the prospect of bankruptcy for both us from the level of 'probable' to, 'Could I outrun the security guard at Tesco?'

Suffering from a paucity of state remuneration, a lack of work, and with what little we were owed almost certainly being spent on tuk-tuks and other cheap rides in Thailand by the senior clerk, life, as they say, was no bowl of cherries.

Jo would oscillate wildly from brilliance to blackness, at times marked by piteous pleas for work, alongside my own, in the vain hope he might be saved from the clutches of financial desolation.

My good friend Stuart, a formidable lawyer and wordsmith, was nothing short of gifted when sober. He had caught his wife in bed with another gentleman and a series of unpleasant incidents, not least an ornate Wedgwood tea-pot being thrown through the living-room window triggered a spot of bother and a spell away from practice. In an attempt to mitigate his melancholia, he had achieved the fertilisation of a beautiful Mediterranean fashion model, which, while on the face of it might be considered to have been at least a little bit therapeutic, showed itself to the contrary during the christening weekend of his newborn.

There had been no interregnum of sobriety over three days, Stuart was hours late for the ceremony and only attended due to the good fortune of his discovery – naked, drunk, sunburnt and mosquito-bitten – in a washed-up fishing boat. The previous evening he had been inconsolable, fighting with the extended family and then making a suicide attempt thwarted by yours truly who dragged him out of the sea at 3am, both naked, in a scene that would have won the leading role in *Brokeback Mountain*. I hear that inner peace is still evading him, a beautiful mind, tortured.

My good friend Tom was so poor that he would sofa-surf if he could find no internet date to put him up for the night. He wouldn't see his wife and kids for weeks on end. His life was one large merry-go-round of boozing and womanising when not in court. As much as it may sound like fun to some, I am convinced that it wasn't. He was a great lawyer and as capable as anybody of bringing in the fish, but he was pursued relentlessly by the black dog.

I would give him the occasional lift to court in my van, always having to collect him from yet another strange address, brothel or the front door of a pub. He became unkempt, the look completed by a Charlie Chaplin suit, holes in his shoes, bleary eyes and the omnipresent stench of booze. Eventually, he failed to show up for court days, even in the middle of important trials. Although the mirror might have shown him a different story, he still possessed the distorted self-belief necessary for the job, believing that he was the misunderstood messiah of greatness, destined to write the next bestseller or be the next music superstar, racing driver, prime minister... The purchasing of a large dildo from a man in the pub as a present for the junior clerk on the premise of a grandiose belief that he was her next intended precipitated his prompt, and final, departure from chambers.

Evan was a close pal in chambers and an adept lawyer. He, like the rest of us, struggled with a lack of work and all the other problems associated with this white-knuckle ride of a job. I am sure that all the late nights working, the lack of money and job-induced personality augmentation did little to arrest his wife's habitual humping of her personal trainer and his life crashing down around his ears. He called me up one day to see if I had any briefs that I could throw his way. He was desperate. I did have one case, and, out of sympathy, I decided that I would let him have it, notwithstanding the resulting dent in my own pocket.

The defendant in the case had been accused of violence and abuse in the street which included obscene and repeated references by him to the victim as a 'stupid, fat, Welsh cunt'. For my friend Evan, a portly and proud Welshman, who hailed from the Rhondda Valleys, it was clear that this case was just the ticket for him, anticipating, as I did, that he would gel with the defendant like a long-lost brother!

It was one of Evan's last cases before he left the bar to seek rehabilitation and alternative employment. Rumour has it that in his state of dejected resignation to fate he said to the jury at the close of his address,

'You may now acquit him, ladies and gentlemen, and this from the mouth of another fat, Welsh cunt. Good day.'

Alistair was one of those members of chambers who would always seem to be knocking about the corridors without any real practice that could be discerned, not that it seemed to make a difference because we were all skint anyway. Between the van and boat accommodation, I stayed with Alistair for a few months at his pokey little flat in South London. He claimed that his OCD forbade my touching of any tea-towels, or the mountain of redundant VCRs, antiquated computer equipment and old papers that occupied the box room from floor to ceiling where I slept. His day consisted of roaming his flat in shorts and slip-on shoes and completing a few levels of *Medal of Honour* on the PlayStation. There were no designated mealtimes that I could see, and when he did eat, the regimen would be the ingestion of four tablespoons of African *chevda* (similar to Bombay mix) and two Quorn cocktail sausages. Occasionally, he might prosecute the odd road-traffic case. We fell out ultimately following a full-on pub brawl between us, triggered by my inflammatory accusation that he had farted on the dance floor. He was perfectly insane.

Rob, at least, had found some contentment in his life, but not by reason of his recent marriage. He had divorced within three months in order to pursue a life of whips, chains and gimp masks in some kind of bondage bonanza. Last I heard, his mouth was zipped up like Zippy's and he was breathing through a straw. They say this had improved his advocacy!

Albeit these were my closest friends, this sort of craziness was the rule, rather than the exception. The longer I have practised, the greater has been my conviction that everyone involved has varying degrees of loose screws, from the local Wolverhampton lad, turned barrister, turned assumed landed gentry from the 1920s, to those wreaking so much like a Christmas pudding that they might be ignited and applauded as they are brought to the table. There is just too great a correlation between talent at the bar and personal chaos for it to be dismissed as a coincidence.

As may already be apparent, the arrow of discontent didn't exactly miss me as a target either. When one becomes engrossed in a good book, there is that moment when the eyes lift from the page and the mind re-engages with reality. Life as a barrister is very much like that. Every case you deal with is a story, or a play with which you become engrossed. You are one of the protagonists, you help compose it, perform it, live it, breathe it. Your imagination guides the ship. But akin to the welder who concentrates so hard on producing a beautiful weld only to lift his darkened welding helmet to discover his shirt sleeve and most of the garage on fire, imagination steps aside to allow for reality, and reality for me was regularly shit street.

Moving from van to boat, to van, to flat of yet another relationship initiated on the internet and terminated with something being thrown at me, the pattern was habitual. For years I lived from a suitcase, seldom unpacking as there seemed little point. I chased the short 'hits', the dopamine highs, passion and happiness: the little bit of juice that nature gives us as a reward for the hard work we don't want to do. Like my friends who stumbled down similar paths, I wanted... needed, to feel a little something of that 'yes!' sensation when the foreperson stands up in a hushed courtroom and announces to the world that I have succeeded in persuading them to see things the way I wanted them to.

It took me more time than seems credible to realise that many of us had been chasing the wrong fox. That selfish and dogged pursuit of 'ups', nature's carrot on a stick, rather than shrewdly investing in contentment, while all the while kicking the can down the road with distractions, be they work, women, drugs or booze, achieves nothing but a ballooning unpaid bill. When, once again, I found myself heartbroken, having discovered that my latest perfidious lover, and home-provider, had shagged her boss at the Christmas party, I took my crappy yellow suitcase in hand and was confronted by the precipice over which I had hung by a fingertip for a long time.

Depression is a curious thing. It will impart its gift of desolation indiscriminately at times, albeit sometimes with a leg-up given by circumstances or life choices. Regardless of one's position in life, what you do or don't have, or what challenges you face, your contentment is limited merely to your perception of it. It is a paradox that those who have nothing, or have to confront exceptional challenges, can often be found to be 'happier' than those that have 'everything'. For me, although relatively 'successful', as measured by certain yardsticks, I didn't feel like I was contributing much good to anything or anyone, and that was part of the problem.

Feeling as if somebody had locked me in a box and thrown both the box and the key into a canal with no prospect of it ever being opened again, I found myself standing in court, desperately trying to maintain the traditional magniloquence, but breaking down in tears. As if that wasn't bad enough, I also experienced anxiety for the first time, so severe that shelving in shops would give me crippling vertigo and I struggled to walk up the street for fear of something, though I had no idea what it was.

Sitting at a train station and staring at the concrete platform for several hours one day was the push I needed to get professional help. It was also time to turn my back on my dissolute city ways, to move away from London and return to the shires, happy, hobbit country. Maybe a concerted effort to find more friends, a home and to step up to the plate as a father would lead me towards more settled times.

# Gloucestershire, the Land of Real Men and Frightened Sheep

There could be no denying that I was delighted to return to my roots in the shires. There was also the added benefit that I was already well acquainted with the local villainy who, upon learning of my return, regularly furnished me with work. Not a day went by that I wasn't called up by one of them for things like selling cocaine, stealing cars or throwing a Filet-O-Fish at people down at the McDonald's drive-through.

This work emanated largely from a local council estate, the tradition of which was the maintenance of an unofficial co-operative designed to furnish the community with anything they wanted. Money was a vulgar subject and would never be discussed let alone exchanged; instead, business would always be conducted on a 'favour-in-hand' basis, or a 'trade-trade'.

The place was headed up by Jay, a shifty character who would speak in double time from the corner of his mouth and be forever looking over his shoulder. He was also exceptionally savvy and, although never involved directly with criminality that I could perceive, he remained firmly on the fringes. He was the connection for anything anyone wanted within the estate, and I was the legal one. To that end, extreme judiciousness in one's expression of desires had to prevail. If, for example, I were to remark that my son wanted a motorbike, a motorbike would be on the doorstep the next day. Similarly, if a roof needed fixing, there would be builders attending to it within the hour, no questions asked and definitely no money exchanged. What was clever about the operation was the subtle creation of indebtedness that would need to be satisfied by the exercise of your own trade. For me this would entail the restoration of liberty for one of the local scrotes who had been caught managing a cannabis factory or driving over somebody at the fish-and-chip shop.

I made the mistake one day of mentioning my son's upcoming birthday and that I was looking to hire a small bouncy castle, did Jay know of anybody? Salvation initially came in the form of 'Mr Tubby', a person located by my mum on the internet who came over in his Ford Mondeo estate complete with trailer and twelve-foot squared inflatable ball pit. Mr Tubby's expression of complete shock and astonishment was shared by all of us when we arrived at my back gate to see that a complete funfair, which towered over the house and spilled out into the adjacent field and public road such was its enormity, had been erected. Goodness knows what sort of villainy underpinned this lot or what debt it would engender. I was at a loss as to what to do, other than to grab Mr Tubby and jump on a waltzer!

On another memorable occasion, the newspapers and the local news broadcasts had reported the burglary of a local firework factory. I mentioned in passing to Jay just what a sad indictment of society it represented, kids going without fireworks on bonfire night because they had been burgled. He bowed his head for a moment in pensive reflection before agreeing wholeheartedly. After another short period of reverie, he looked up and said, 'Do you want any rockets?'

Suffice to say that the skies over the council estate that bonfire night were nothing short of a pyrotechnic tour de force.

## Fight at the Chippy – Two Fish, a Sausage, and a Local Lad got Battered

Talking of running people over at the local fish-and-chip shop, those were the facts pertaining to the first case I dealt with on my return to the shires. Mr K, on discovering his sweetheart in a bedroom clinch with another local lad, pursued his love rival up the road in his car as the philanderer tried to make good his escape. The escapee did a relatively good job, in fairness, but the wall of the Chinese takeaway/fish-and-chip shop in combination with the awesome power of the V-reg Ford Fiesta proved too formidable an opponent. My client ran him over without a moment's hesitation.

At the Gloucester Crown Court a truly delightful judge welcomed me.

'You are not from around here are you. London?'

I briefly explained to His Honour my circumstances.

'Well this is how we do it in Gloucester,' he said. 'On one view, your client, discovering his girlfriend in bed with the complainant, pursued him and deliberately ran him over at Tony Wong's chip shop. Another view is that he accidently slipped on the accelerator, inadvertently rendering the complainant vulnerable to the forward movement of the car. The question for me is, which view should be preferred?'

At that point I could have assisted the Judge in his resolution of the facts by pointing out that Mr D had been run over twice. The latter view would presuppose that my client had engaged first gear, slipped on the clutch, slipped on the accelerator before re-engaging the clutch, selecting reverse, slipping on the clutch again and then slipping on the accelerator one final time. That was a lot of accidental slippage in a single sitting. Discretion being the better part of valour, however, I resolved simply to nod my head earnestly.

'I have decided that the appropriate view to take is the latter. This was an unfortunate incident the likes of which I doubt will be repeated again. The defendant shall be released subject to a suspended sentence.'

My client, complete with rucksack containing articles in preparation for an anticipated four-year holiday at Her Majesty's pleasure, walked out of court a free man, making me a local hero amongst the crims.

## Steroids Warehouse

It wasn't long before I was back again, this time representing the proprietor of 'Steroids Warehouse'. I wondered what could possibly have attracted the attention of the authorities to this particular discerning businessman, but anyway, it seemed that the police had got it into their heads, for some reason, that he might be associated with the supply of steroids. On raiding his property, the police not only found enough steroids to turn an army of Walter the Softys into Magnús Ver Magnússons, they also found a Chinese-made electric stun gun disguised as a torch.

It was not clear whether this thing actually worked or, even if it did, how effective it was. Such devices are not considered lethal or even particularly harmful, especially compared to something like a knife, but, to cut a long story sideways, the courts have interpreted the firearms legislation to apply to electric stun guns. The consequence of that is if you are caught in possession of one, you are exposed to a statutory minimum sentence of five years' imprisonment, unless the court can be persuaded that exceptional circumstances would justify another course. The drugs business was not the problem. The sentence for that would be dwarfed by the one imposed for this crappy little stun gun. In these types of cases, for reasons that might be obvious, defence teams do their best to provide the judge with an avenue to some discretion on the minimum-sentence provisions.

When explaining all of this to my client, he queried whether he should suggest that the stun gun belonged to his girlfriend, thus proffering an 'exceptional circumstance' that could divert the judge from the minimum term. It was a demonstrable lie, no doubt, but if those were his instructions, then that was the case I could fight. Besides, I also thought it was quite a good wheeze. Given that this judge had already proved himself a sympathetic pragmatist, he might be only too happy to avoid a sentence that any right-thinking person would regard as objectionably incommensurate with the crime.

Reassured that he needn't concern himself with media reporting – no journalist worth his salt would be interested in what was a comparatively minor case – my client braced himself for the proceedings. With his full endorsement, we proceeded headlong with our shenanigans and, despite the judge giving me a definite look as if to say, 'I threw you a bone last time but that doesn't give you carte blanche to completely take the piss,' he was nevertheless receptive. It wasn't until that evening that a hiccup made itself known.

Jay invited me to join him at the client's home, in part to explain the outcome of the day's proceedings to the client's girlfriend, but also to revel in a bit of glory from the success. Stood in the kitchen with my client, his girlfriend and Jay, I began proudly to explain the methodology behind my mastery and the agreeable consequences that flowed from that mastery, leaving out one or two inconsequential details about who we had to blame to get there. It was during the course of said gloating that Jay, who had been concurrently reading the local rag, exclaimed that the case had been reported, words that instantaneously stunned me and made my blood freeze.

'Read it out!' insisted the defendant's girlfriend excitedly.

Even though Jay had caught my eye and aptly read my body language which screamed, 'DON'T!', it was too late. He had begun. 'Despite his guilty pleas to all charges,' he announced uneasily, gulping heavily, 'the local drug baron corrected the court that the firearm discovered in his chest of drawers was not his…'

Jay paused and looked around nervously at the expectant faces.

'Can you read it?' he said to me, hastily throwing the paper in my direction.

I tossed it back at him like a hot potato, simultaneously making a beeline for the door.

I wished Jay had had the foresight to make something up, but he was obviously an amateur under pressure. Grabbing the paper out of his hands, my client's girlfriend read the rest of the article aloud. It proceeded not only to name her and give her home address, but also, in effect, to put her name up in lights as ' Billy the Kid', the notorious gun-slinger of the west.

Jay and I already knew that this now reputed firearm possessor had a fearsome reputation for being a trifle 'fizzy', and it was for that reason that I already had my hand on the door. I can tell you that I have encountered angrier people, but I really can't remember when. I have struggled to find the best words to aptly describe her reaction to her new-found fame, and eventually settled on these: she went absolutely fucking mental.

It seems that by some miracle my client retained his life long enough to attend his sentencing hearing, wherein the judge gave him two years in the hole. He wrote to me from prison and thanked me for my efforts, remarking that, for him, custody was a marked improvement on his home life with the missus. His only regret about the whole thing was that he had been given only two years, not a minimum of five!

## Stupidity is his Best Point

In another spectacular bit of justice at the provincial crown courts, the judge, in sentencing the co-defendant in a drugs case, reflected that the defendant's 'utter stupidity' justified a lesser sentence and that if he wanted to 'rot his brain stem out' with cannabis, then his inherent brainlessness was an affliction comprising punishment in itself.

There was very little that was positive to say on my client's behalf in mitigation and, having heard this, I jumped on the bandwagon when it was my turn to speak. The judge saw great force in my argument that my client, too, possessed the mental agility of an escaped gust of flatulence and that being a complete moron was undoubtedly his best point. I went as far as to suggest, with respect, that my client's status as a pre-eminent sub-normal should surely be a basis for an even greater discount in deciding the sentencing tariff. The judge agreed.

## Casual Incest

It is interesting how the law and court practice symbiotically adapt to prevailing cultural attitudes. For example, the decriminalising of homosexuality or the abolition of the right to physically chastise one's wife represent progressive shifts consistent with the ever-changing societal status quo. Similarly, in times of increased incidences of certain types of crime, such as the possession of knives in public, court practice adapts to the interests of the public they serve.

The plasticity of the provincial courts similarly lends itself to the will of their local communities, but it is only when one leaves the London courts for the sticks that one realises that approaches to certain types of offending are not nationally uniform.

Take Hereford Crown Court as a case in point. In London there would doubtless be little interest in a case of one farmer stealing a bullock belonging to his neighbour. It probably wouldn't even be a priority, taking its place in a queue behind murders, rapes or frauds. In the countryside town of Hereford, however, one such case sent the local media into a frenzy. The trial and subsequent sentencing made the war crimes trial of Radovan Karadžić look like *Topsy and Tim at the Fairground*.

Whilst the courts of Herefordshire regard farming trespasses as the apical violation of our moral fabric, the occasional sympathies of Gloucester Crown Court give their own intriguing insights into the differing regional conscience of my new home. I have in mind the case of Mrs X.

Mrs X was in her fifties when she was caught having sex with her teenage son. In furtherance of their collective design, and I say collective because each protagonist was as eager as the other to participate in behaviour that was ostensibly consensual, Mrs X would dress up in thigh boots and a PVC basque bought for her by her son on eBay. Leaving aside for a moment how the perusal of romantic text messages between them evoked within me, as it would in any normal person, an irresistible urge to vomit violently up a nearby wall, I had rather anticipated the courts would take a dim view of Mrs X and her son's antics. That proved, however, to be a product of my metropolitan prejudices, as the judge declined even to pass an immediate sentence of imprisonment.

In passing sentence, the judge delivered a carefully crafted edict. The thrust of his contemplations were dressed up in niceties to the extent that I merely summarise the gist of his argument, as I suppose it to be. To imprison someone in this jurisdiction for incest would be akin to incarcerating someone for dressing a well in Malvern, rolling a cheese on Coopers Hill or playing football in the river at Bourton-on-the-Water. All localities have their peculiar traditions stretching back to time immemorial. Who were the courts, therefore, to defrock those engaged in the time-hallowed recreational practices of Mitcheldean?

# Welcome to Mordor

It was a source of real regret that the majority of my work was not centred in Gloucester which, for reasons I am sure you can understand, is a place I hold dear in my heart. Most of my time was spent in Birmingham and the surrounding region.

With the exception of the flirtatious court usher who would record my name on the court list as Mr NL (Nice Looking), the subject matter of frequent 'discussions' between us in the privacy of a conference room, the West Midlands was otherwise unalluring. If working there was the path to the wholesome edification I was seeking, then it wasn't exactly making itself known, at least not initially. Having worked in London for sixteen years, I didn't really have many contacts there. I found myself working for a very shonky set of chambers, where my co-workers, while honest, were chaotic. Unlike the big chambers which had embraced digital technology, this one emphatically hadn't. A paper diary ensured that hearings were missed, which pissed off the solicitors and the courts alike. The judiciary were hostile to outsiders, and the only solicitors who would instruct me were crooks. It seemed that the Midlands was suffused with them, all bending and manipulating the legal-aid system until the pips squeaked, and encouraging their instructed barristers to do their dirty work. If you weren't prepared to dance to their tune, then you wouldn't get their work.

A footnote here on dodgy solicitors, now that I have raised this issue. After all, a memoir of the privations of a jobbing barrister would be incomplete without mention of the travails one faces on a frequent basis courtesy of the manipulations of these tyrants.

To an extent, they have been the product of how the 'legal aid funding structure' has been vulnerable to exploitation. Traditionally, both solicitors and barristers would be paid with reference to the numbers of pages of evidence served in a case. It follows that there was always much eagerness to receive the paper-heavy cases, whether barrister or solicitor, because they paid much better. It eventually dawned on the Ministry of Justice and those tasked with the question of efficiency savings, that by reason of inadequate scrutiny of what paperwork was being categorised as 'evidence', and by the constructive design, or indifference, of the payees, lawyers were being paid a lot of money for stuff that was never read and, in reality, would never feature in the trial.

The ultimate solution was to stop paying barristers on a page-by-page basis and instead pay them a set fee.

This shifted the burden to the barrister to argue, with documentary support, for an enhanced fee if significantly more work had been undertaken than might have been envisaged for a 'standard case' of that type. It has resulted, largely, in a much fairer system. Having said that, not only do many of the bigger cases now not pay anything like they did before, but, like any indiscriminate approach, made worse here by impenetrable billing bureaucracy, barristers can also find themselves settling for a lot less remuneration than would be considered reasonable for their true input on some paper-heavy cases. The unforeseen net effect of all of this was that, suddenly, the 'big hitters' in chambers, never previously celebrated for their 'generous spirit' within the brotherhood when it came to the distribution of work, took to charitably giving their heavy cases to the lesser mortals, like me. And, while they were at it, would take all of the little cases, formerly regarded as the 'shite', for themselves in an apparent complete reversal of the prior trend.

You are soon to enjoy my reminiscences of a six-week stint in Wales, very much a case in point. I was happy, though, to work for less if it meant that, finally, we could all just get on with the job and dispense with the delays and stresses in cases caused by cynical arguments made by lawyers, the topics of which were guided, not by the interests of their clients, but rather whether material in the case should be categorised as 'evidence' or 'unused material'. That wish, sadly, has not become a reality because solicitors are still paid with reference to 'pages of evidence served'.

Here is your profile of the archetypal 'dodgy' solicitor. He will sell fantasies of liberty to his prospective clientele, often the pre-existing clients of decent solicitors who have, hitherto, offered a more pessimistic, but honest prediction. He will do little work on the case, instead dumping everything on the barrister. When it comes to the trial, the solicitor will attend with his client to ensure that the barrister does not tell him the truth about his prospects lest it result in a less lucrative guilty plea. And then there is the issue of the 'page count'. To give an example, if a drugs prosecution relies in part on a few text messages found during a trawl of a mobile phone which itself generated an additional three-thousand pages of useless gobbledygook, the solicitor will apply pressure to their barrister to prevent agreement between the parties which would allow only the relevant messages to be put before the jury. Instead, they will insist that the whole mobile-phone report is adduced. That is, of course, unless the three-thousand pages of unused material is simply renamed 'evidence' for billing purposes, in which case the trial can proceed in whichever agreed, fair and efficient way counsel and the judge wish.

At the end of the case, when the overwhelming evidence unsurprisingly convicts the defendant, who is as a result disgruntled and has some questions for his solicitors, they are gone – back to a prison to blow more smoke and empty promises up the arses of those on remand – leaving counsel to deal with the fallout.

I have had solicitors sit in conferences with the client and me at court and shamelessly tell the client to ignore everything I have said of his prospects and that he should fight the case to its conclusion. Even judges occasionally capitulate to the will of the solicitors and order that clearly irrelevant documentation is classified as 'evidence' out of desperation to avoid delays and keep the assault going on the ever-increasing backlog of cases. There are barristers that bend to the will of these charlatans, feeling unable to tell them to 'fuck off', as I now do, because without their instructions they wouldn't be paying the bills.

The immediate resolution to this is to stop paying solicitors on a 'page count' basis and for the Solicitors Regulation Authority to go after these bad eggs relentlessly until they are gone.

That is not to say that there aren't some solicitors who are brilliant, honest, hard-working and who play with a straight bat. I love to work with them. But for those I have previously described, I will be swilling out the khazis with my shirt sleeve at the local irritable bowel walk-in centre long before I step within a mile of them again. If the Midlands is representative of the national percentage, I just hope that if we ever do manage to rid the system of the dead wood and rotten fruit, there is something left of the tree.

# The View From the Other Side

For reasons that may be apparent, I began focusing much more on prosecuting and, in particular, increasingly large volumes of sex cases. They were getting to me a bit, too, not just the distressing nature of many of them but the additional pressure, which was inherent in them.

One particular case that sticks in the mind was that of Mr H. The case came to me as a re-trial after a previous jury had been unable to decide on the defendant's guilt. I was instructed to take over the reins and give it a try. I am not going to use the word 'alleged' because even though he ultimately got away with it, through hard-earned intuition, I know when a defendant is guilty, and he was.

The accused was an obese, bespectacled and perspiring gentleman in his late forties. He was a loner, estranged from his wife and children, which at least gave him more time to indulge in his pastime of internet perusal. There was no doubt that he welcomed the re-establishment of contact with his kids, particularly that of his ten-year-old daughter who was given special privileges, which included washing her father's pudgy naked torso in the shower at his bedsit and sharing his bed at night. He also raped her, regularly. She reported, among other disturbing behaviours, how she would sometimes awaken to find her father sitting in a chair staring longingly at her.

The defence challenged her doggedly, not in an overtly aggressive way, or in breach of the rules, but in a way that appealed to the many stereotypes of how a victim of sexual abuse reacts post trauma. For example, they referred to records of her disruptive and sometimes dishonest behaviour when in the care of the social services to good effect for the defence. The truth was that all of the victim's behaviour was classically symptomatic of a young victim of abuse.

Mercifully, much progress has been made in recent years to guide the jury with our better understanding of victim behaviour, but, of course, with due care not to interfere with their ability properly to interrogate the evidence. My grievance this time was less with the conduct of the defence and more with the jury's stupidity, which had, once again, prevailed. I am sure that I was only a whisker away from a verdict but clearly at least three jurors, much to the obvious exasperation and anger of the others, remained unconvinced.

Two trials without a verdict usually equates to a throwing in of the towel, which is what I had little choice but to do here. I wasn't going to allow the unpersuaded jurors to leave court and sleep soundly that night though. In the guise of an inane submission before they departed, I referred to the evidence which had come to light so late that the judge had ruled it inadmissible in the trial and of which, up until now, the jury had remained ignorant. It was with some satisfaction, then, that I witnessed the colour drain from their faces as I revealed the defendant's internet search history which included the search terms 'sex with daughter when asleep'.

On the other side of the coin, over-zealous interference in cases can lead directly to miscarriages of justice. When defending a rape case in Luton, for example, my greatest battle was with the judge, who felt that I was 'stereotyping' and deploying excessively vehement cross-examination. Had she succeeded in her attempt to curtail my challenge of the witness, an innocent man would have been convicted in the face of an initially convincing case. Eventually the truth came out, but only via dextrous circumnavigation of Her Honour's restrictions, with which she had inadvertently imperilled justice. The complainant had been experiencing paranoid delusions, which became apparent when she alluded to a belief that the defendant was just one of a hundred or so men who would break into her accommodation nightly and rape her while she slept.

The expressions on the jurors' faces changed in an instant from scowls of distaste for the defendant complete with crossed arms to horrified looks of 'Oh shit, we almost convicted this bloke'. He was lucky; some are less fortunate.

As is common at the Bar, sometimes you are ahead, sometimes you are behind, but a further frustrating series of failed cases began to instil some real disillusionment in me. Two further cases I defended in close proximity of each other were the capstone of the most dismal time for me at the Bar, and both were during my early nomadic period in the West Midlands.

The first related to a gentleman who had been charged with the rape of a prostitute. He had at least been given a fairish trial the first time round, but an undecided jury resulted in a retrial. At the end of any trial, after speeches by the prosecution and defence, the judge will sum up the case for the jury. He or she will give directions on the law and a conspectus of the facts. Judges are entitled, to an extent, to express their own view on the strengths and weaknesses of the evidence. A defence barrister will always expect and prepare for the contingency that a judge will be overtly sympathetic towards the prosecution, as is very often the case. The learned recorder in this trial, however, cognizant of weaknesses in the prosecution case brought to the fore through endless hours of my own hard work, not only failed to highlight any positive points for the defence, but blatantly misrepresented the prosecution case to the extent that any semblance of fairness went firmly out of the window.

I am pretty sure, by the measure of the intensity of our courtroom exchanges when the jury was not present, the judge was left under no illusion as to the extent of my regret that he had ever been born, but the jury, being the jury, through misguided esteem for the judge, were accordingly bent to his unconscionable perspective. In my humble opinion, an innocent man was convicted and continues to serve a long prison sentence.

The Court of Appeal initially suggested that my arguments were without merit and refused leave to appeal. My strong sense that an injustice had been done nevertheless drove me to pursue the appeal on a *pro bono* basis. At a full hearing at the Court of Appeal my arguments were found to be 'well placed', but the conviction was nonetheless upheld. My client still protests his innocence.

The second pertained to a man I defended, similarly charged with sex offences. I had unearthed evidence of collusion, a motive for the complainants to fabricate their accounts, as well as evidence of witness coaching. In addition, one of the complainants had previously made a complaint of sexual assault against somebody else, which had proceeded to a trial and concluded with an acquittal of the accused. The presiding judge prevented me from articulating any of this material before the jury. To make matters worse, the judge demanded lists of my proposed questions for the witnesses prior to the commencement of the trial and then edited them to an extent that made them significantly less effectual. As if that wasn't enough, she endlessly intervened in my cross-examination and the manner in which she did so can only have left an impression on the jury that she was entirely contemptuous of the efforts of the defence. The cherry on the cake was her résumé of the evidence, which I'm sure you can picture. My client was convicted and sent to prison for fifteen years. The Court of Appeal upheld the conviction.

Having done the job for so many years, I have a very good feel for where the truth lies. It is mercifully seldom that I worry that a jury has got it wrong. My client here didn't have a fair trial and, to compound that, I am not sure he did it. He, too, continues to protest his innocence.

By this time in my career, I was tired and disenchanted. It wasn't just the recent adverse results, but all of the battles and the confrontations, both professional and not so professional, that had taken it out of me.

The same day that that case finished, I caught the train home from court, pulled my motorcycle out from the shed and set off on a ride to blow away the cobwebs. I also blew away my leg and hand, my final memory of that week being the view of a car roof from a height of about three feet. The next was of polystyrene ceiling tiles at the local hospital. A broken leg was going to keep me there for some time and a very damaged hand signified the end of my guitar-playing days.

They tell you it doesn't matter if the chips are down. One must seize the opportunities as they present themselves. For my steady girlfriend at the time, who lovingly visited me with uplifting little treats, her opportunity presented itself due to my plastered leg being strapped to the hospital ceiling until a future date to be confirmed. It was jarring news that, not unlike the Easter bunny, she had during my incarceration also done much to uplift the spirits of her ex-boyfriend, the plumber, the postman, the builder, and ten soldiers down at the local army barracks, too.

The question for me was whether I would brush myself off and walk away (speaking metaphorically, of course), with my head held high, or whether I was too jaded and lacking any modicum of self-respect to do anything other than invite another shot of morphine from my medical team. 'Nurse!'

My mind turned to a friend of my dad who came over to our house one evening some years ago. He had lost everything. His boss had handed him his hat, his wife had caught him fully clothed from the waist up in the company of the au pair and had flushed his car keys down the toilet, and the bank had foreclosed on his house. He was in floods of tears.

'Don't worry, Dave,' said my dad, embracing him warmly as he imparted sage advice to his old friend. 'When you are down, flat on your back, old boy, you can't fall off the floor!'

It was less than twelve hours later that my dad received a telephone call from the cardiac ward at Bristol Infirmary. It was Dave. He had had a heart attack.

'John, it's me, Dave,' he said. 'I think I have just fallen through the floor.'

I had some empathy for how it might feel, falling through the floor. When you have shouldered the burden of unfairness in the courts, when the world hates you, when some clown of a registrar has stitched your finger on back to front, when your girlfriend's coital philanthropy has nurtured twelve men, their dogs and a bottle of pop down at the meadow, you tend to feel a little... piqued.

With my personal life feeling about as appealing as a bag of dog poo hanging from a bush, my bitterness manifested itself as a ripping up of the carpet in the courts. I didn't care much for being screwed over again and, frankly, it didn't matter to me if you were a road sweeper or His Excellency Lord Smithers of Smithersville. If you were going to try to knock me down again, I was fully intent on rising like a serpent, dislocating my jaw and consuming your corpse – whole.

## Just Don't Ask Him Those Questions

I was prosecuting a threats-to-kill matter at the Worcester Crown Court.

It was said by the prosecution that, during his stay in prison, the defendant had sent innumerable letters and made numerous telephone calls in which he had made the most graphic promises to bring an untimely end to his father's life. There was no genuine motive for it, actually. The defendant was just a horrible dick.

As is the convention, I had a chat in the robing room pre-trial with a very well-disposed barrister who had attended to represent the accused. He told me that he was still relatively new to the profession, formerly having worked as a journalist for one of the national papers. As we considered the case and our trial strategy, he implored me not to broach the subject of the defendant's hatred of his father, and instead to direct my focus elsewhere. He speculated that to do otherwise would cause the defendant to become very 'riled up'.

Dirty Briefs

I looked at him with some wonderment, it seldom being the case that a defence barrister would provide information to a prosecutor that could be used to demonstrate to a jury the volatility of a man who was accused of being, well, volatile. I nodded my head perfidiously in the certain knowledge that I was going to take full advantage of this information as soon as the opportunity arose. I didn't feel bad for the defence counsel. I was planning to stab him in the back, true, but it would be merely an obstacle in the way for my opponent on the long road that we all must tread towards competency. Besides, this defendant was an animal and the more efficiently I could dispatch him, the better.

In his evidence, the defendant was astonishingly unpleasant and combative despite the relatively gentle nature of the questioning at the outset. Halfway through my cross-examination, I decided to drop the bomb and explore the *verboten* topic.

For what he lacked in savviness, he made up for in perspicacity. My learned opponent had been more than accurate in his predictions of aberrant unfriendliness. The nature of the resulting outburst, replete with plentiful 'fucks' and 'cunts', required an urgent taking of cover behind the lectern and an eye to my potential escape route: over two benches and a cardboard box to the door.

The one dream that every lawyer has, which very, very seldom ever comes true, is to wring a mid-testimony confession from a witness. Today, despite the terrifying circumstances, my dream came true… The defendant turned to the jury from the witness box and said:

'Yeah, I fucking did it, and I meant it, too. When I get out of here that cunt is going to get stabbed.'

He then looked towards his barrister and in the style of the great Lord Sugar said, accusatorily:

'This is all your fucking fault, dickhead. You're fired!'

As he did so, he lobbed a plastic cup from the edge of the witness box towards his counsel, the aerodynamics of which caused it to swerve violently from its intended trajectory and bounce off the forehead of an innocent CPS paralegal three rows back. The jury collectively leant away from the witness box in terror; defence counsel may as well have jumped into my arms and clung to my neck, such was the air of pants-wetting. The judge, on the other hand, did not so much as bat an eyelid.

'It appears that Mr J has dispensed with your services,' he said, composedly.

With that, defence counsel scampered hastily out of court and the trial continued in his absence.

The judge was an old boy from the old school who had seen it all over the years; it would take a great deal to ruffle his feathers, but I had supposed he might at least have been tempted to hold the defendant in contempt of court. Somewhat taken aback at his apparent indifference to the outburst, I gathered my thoughts and proceeded with my cross-examination, albeit with a little more circumspection in the interest of my future health. In response to the majority of questions the reply was, 'I don't give a shit, this is a poxy case anyway.'

The inevitable conviction that followed was met with an immediate sentence. For the offence itself, unembellished by the throwing of cups, sacking of lawyers and utterances of 'cunts', 'fucks' and 'poxiness', not to mention promises of death, I would have expected a sentence somewhere in the region of eighteen months or so. With the same serenity and courtesy that had been his hallmarks throughout the trial, the judge handed down his award.

'For this poxy case, you shall go to prison for six years.'

## I Haven't Read It

I was co-defending with a solicitor advocate in a trial that had been thrown my way at the last minute by the clerks. I was representing the first defendant and he the second. He skipped over to me enthusiastically in the advocates room to chat about the case. He seemed like a nice guy and was clearly well prepared.

'What do you think of the evidence of X?' he enquired. 'Do you think we should take an admissibility argument on Y?' he asked. 'Do you think we should argue the identification parade out?' he continued.

'Woah! Woah! Woah! Let me stop you right there, sheriff!' I interrupted. 'I haven't read a bean of this pile of shite and have not a clue what is going on. You will have to give me five minutes. I suspect very much that these cowboy solicitors, whoever they are, have done fuck all too.'

I pondered for a moment as to who my instructing solicitor actually was: the point at which jellification of my limbs took hold. In a classic 'he's behind me, isn't he?' moment, I said, '*You* are my instructing solicitor, aren't you?'

Fuck.

## Motorboating on the Masseuse

I am a staunch defender of individual autonomy, the usurping of which is manifest in assaults against the person, but – call me beastly – I just couldn't help feeling a little sympathy for the local imam convicted of 'motorboating' on a masseuse's breasts. Every man has needs, but great caution need be exercised to ensure that the meeting of those needs is with the full consent of any other party. This is where he had fallen foul of the law.

Having enjoyed what he had assumed to be an 'executive massage', complete with 'happy ending', the ending was, as fate would have it, altogether many times less happy than predicted. As the much revered pillar of society rolled over following a good, oily rub-down, he began blowing a few raspberries on the masseuse's breasts and juggling them mercilessly as if performing an impressive circus act. She took a little umbrage by all accounts. In fact, she called the cops.

A thoughtful employee in the court listing office had listed the case before the only Muslim judge in the court centre who, unsurprisingly, proceeded to throw the book at the defendant, castigating him severely for bringing shame on the faith. I understood his view, but my own liberalism made me feel that had my client simply asked me for recommendations before mistakenly stumbling into the establishment he had chosen, the whole experience would have been a great deal 'happier', and decidedly less criminal.

## Nice Face

I had some advice for my client. 'If you are ever of a mind to surreptitiously video the buxom au pair again as she takes a shower then:

a. Resist. It is unlawful.
b. If you ignore 'a', then don't have the camera recording your eager face as you set it up because the footage will tend to hint at the perpetrator. Nob.

## Satisfied by the Sight of Soap Suds

Given that solicitors get more money when cases proceed to a full trial, as opposed to when they are resolved by means of an admission of guilt, the bandits who had instructed me on this one had persuaded the client that he had a good case worth fighting.

He had been accused of videoing his stepdaughter in the shower. His defence was that out of concern for the personal hygiene of his daughter, he had installed a secret video camera in the bathroom, blue-toothed to his laptop next door, in order to check that she was washing herself appropriately. The point on the footage where it zooms in on her pubic area was part of the operation to look for soap suds. Satisfied that soap suds were indeed present, the camera zoomed back out.

I like to remain on friendly terms with instructing solicitors, and I am more prepared than most to be laughed out of town in the name of earning my crust, but bugger me if I was going to stand there and argue this nonsense to a jury.

'What do you think of my prospects?' my client asked.

'Come on, mate!'

# It's Behind You

As able a spokesman as I may be, organisation has never been my strong point if I am truly honest with myself. At school, no kid would ever sit next to me in art class or science because paper and paint and sulphuric acid and methyl benzoate and a whole raft of other shit would be going off all over the place. This weakness, sadly, persisted into adulthood.

My trial notes and case papers tend to be scattered to the four winds. Speeches and cross-examination questions would be scribbled indecipherably on the back of files, or scraps of paper, circled and arrowed with annotations and scribblings out. My head was like a box of fireworks going off simultaneously and chaos was simply the product of the way I worked. Despite the unholy mess that belied my fluent orations, my skills were sufficient to blind the judge and jury to my disorganisation.

On this occasion, half-way through my speech to the jury in an attempted murder trial, I was desperately hunting for my notes from the cross-examination. I knew that they were somewhere in the clutter on the bench, but couldn't quite put my finger on them. Being the master of disguise and the experienced rhetorician I was, my sleight of hand succeeded in maintaining the jury's ignorance of the lost notes, despite my increasing panic. It was serendipitous, I thought, for a note to be passed to the judge from the jury bringing about a pause in proceedings at precisely the moment I needed one for a secret search for the missing document.

'Pause there for a moment, may we please,' said the judge. 'The jury have passed up a note.' Handing the piece of paper to the court clerk, the judge said, 'Please give this to counsel for their consideration, defence first.'

The note read: 'Please advise defence counsel that the notes he is looking for can be located under the blue lever-arch file on top of the lectern.'

## More Holes Than My Learned Friend's Crotch

To cause no fewer than two senior members of the Bar, where the convention is to display at least a façade of respect to their fellow barristers, to independently liken my outward appearance to a 'colossal bag of shit', probably takes some doing. To say that I had not resented this foul description, or that I was not deserving of it, would be paltering with the truth. A glance in the mirror revealing the image of a battered-looking figure adorned with a disintegrating wig, torn gown, mismatched jacket, suit trousers replete with yoghurt stain and brown shoes unsuccessfully disguised with black boot polish, arguably left me little latitude for disputing this description.

But you know how it is with these things. The wound heals and the agony abates, particularly if one is able to project one's insecurities onto another deserving contender. This victim came in the form of my learned friend for the prosecution, who, by the time of his weekend mishap with a matrimonial campfire, had been prosecuting a case for several weeks in which I and five others appeared for the defence.

On the day of the speeches it could barely go unnoticed that he had arrived at court with an obvious absence where the crotch of his trousers had once been. The explanation, when he was challenged on this, was that in a state of inebriation he had stumbled too close to a fire pit at the wedding he had been attending on the Saturday night, the unfortunate consequence of which was the ignition of his trousers. Unperturbed, his judicious use of a fire extinguisher had allowed him to continue with the festivities, and for his suit trousers, arguably, to survive to fight another day.

My learned friend's contention that his trousers had, *quidem*, survived the blaze, was in truth a point of conjecture, hotly debated by his opponents. For my own part, I considered that prosecution suggestions to a jury that they had a cut-and-dried case was audacious enough, but as nothing compared to its representative rising to his hind legs to address twelve laypeople as to the solemnity of the occasion while sporting a pair of trousers refashioned by fire into something resembling a pair of riding chaps.

'Members of the jury,' I bellowed, in the plumbiest voice I could muster, 'The prosecution case has as many holes as my learned friend's crotch!'

The guy positioned at the end of the jury box pointed, the woman in the centre of the second row reached for her spectacles, the judge raised his hand to his face. They all nodded. Four verdicts of guilty for the co-defendants but one of not guilty for me. There could be no doubt that the defence case lacked any substance, but this barrister was right. Nothing compared to the vacuity of the prosecution's trousers.

**I Am a Fat Bastard, I Am a Fat Bastard, I Am a Fat Bastard**
I found myself entangled in a nasty, 'cut-throat' defence that was even beginning to get personal between the barristers. There were two defendants, both of whom had been charged with various offences of neighbourhood unpleasantness. I represented the first.

It was said that my chap had, among other things, attempted to stab the second defendant with a kitchen knife in response to the first defendant having mixed up a broth of crushed Scotch-bonnet chillies and spraying it in his eyes from a washing-up liquid bottle. Each defendant denied his own particular outrage, but agreed with the prosecution as to the wrongdoing of the other.

We were two weeks in before reaching the case of the second defendant, Mr J, largely owing to him having been so pissed every day in court that he would pass out unconscious in the dock and need to be taken to hospital by the afternoon.

With similar commitment, I had regularly requested the production of the T-shirt that Mr J had been wearing at the time of the offences. If he had been stabbed, as he fancifully claimed, we would surely see some damage to the garment. The fact that the prosecution had not mentioned this T-shirt since, despite my persistent requests for it to be produced, was probably suggestive that it was as right as ninepence, and exonerative. Smelling prosecutorial subterfuge, I very vocally implored the judge, and police, to get it to court forthwith. In fact, a day didn't go by that I didn't renew my request.

My focus on this particular morning, though, was on the evidence of the co-defendant Mr J, who was arguably sober enough to take the stand; in other words, he hadn't fallen over backwards by midday.

I wouldn't be so generous as to say that his testimony was intelligible, but no one could deny that, at least initially, some of the words emitted from his mouth loosely resembled the English language. He was about twenty minutes in when he suddenly, and curiously, resigned himself to a form of words which he, at that point and henceforth, used to answer every question that the prosecutor posed to him: 'I am a fat bastard.'

The judge looked up and appeared a little perplexed, but about three further questions were allowed, each resulting in the same answer, before he intervened.

'Stop that, stop that at once, I implore you! You are invited to attest to what you saw and heard, and not to otherwise use expletives or make irrelevant remarks.'

The questioning continued and it was only a short while before the defendant resumed his folly, answering every question with, 'I am a fat bastard'.

Nobody could fathom what benefit there might be in answering in such a way, other than avoiding an uncomfortable silence for want of a cogent answer, but then again, maybe it was pointless to attempt to rationalise the utterances of a man so heavily intoxicated.

'Mr J,' said the prosecutor, 'you heard what the judge said, please focus on the question rather than self-descriptive curses.'

Further questions were posed, which all elicited the reply, 'I am a fat bastard'.

Observing, as we all did, that Mr J was indeed fat, and doubtless a bastard, and through exasperation that his case was not being progressed with anything approaching expediency, the prosecutor provoked a 'quiet talking to' from the judge, ex parte, for this response to the latest outburst from the defendant:

'I am not denying it, Mr J, now just answer the question!'

In the break that was ordered to allow for judicial admonishment of the prosecutor for his publicly implied sympathy for the second defendant's self-description, the police detective threw a paper evidence bag over to me on the side of the court. I opened it to discover the T-shirt that

I had been requesting all along. I unrolled it and examined it, holding it up to the light to reveal more holes than a Swiss-cheese, post firing squad.

Looking over my shoulder, I could see that everybody else was preoccupied with other matters and hadn't noticed the significant 'unravelling' that was occurring at the end of the bench. With hasty discernment, I folded it up and stuffed it back in the bag.

Nothing to see here!

## For the Good of Gotham City

I felt it prudent to desist in my plea in mitigation to draw parallels between villainy in Gotham City and the pursuit of investment banking in a bid to minimise the culpability of my client Robin who, in concert with Batman and the Green Lantern, decisively kicked the shit out of some Barclays' employees at the fancy-dress Christmas party. I did manage to allow some tumble-weed into the court, though, when I observed that the police were still looking for The Invisible Man.

## British Upskirt Panty Pervert

People plead not guilty for a variety of reasons. Maybe they are innocent? (Unusual.) Maybe they don't want to face the truth? Maybe the prosecution evidence is inadequate to prove the case against them? One further possibility that shouldn't be overlooked is that the defence barrister has not read the case sufficiently to appreciate just how screwed their client really is to then be able to convey this information to the client.

This was the situation in the case of Mr D who had been identified indulging in a bit of 'upskirting'. With a camera mounted on his shoe and, at other times, adopting the less furtive technique of diving beneath the pleats of the general public's outer garments, he trod his path to euphoric titillation, and prosecution.

I was presenting the case on behalf of the Crown and was rather miffed at having to do so. Had the defendant been my client, I would have just told him to plead guilty and be done with it, but sadly not all defence barristers are as lucid as I am. If they were, I would have been at home long ago with a Jaffa cake and mug of tea watching *Cash in the Attic* and not, as I was, organising jury bundles and formal admissions of fact.

'Why the fuck is your client fighting this?' I asked the defence barrister politely. 'He is bollocksed!'

I had well anticipated some defence intransigence but maybe not the degree of po-faced righteousness that underscored his reply.

'Maybe because you haven't got one shred of evidence that corroborates the supposed identification by these two women,' he said forthrightly.

I wondered for a moment whether we were at cross purposes here or if we were even talking about the same case. I directed his attention to the case papers.

'What about the two-hundred-and-five photographs on his phone, one or two depicting more conservative petticoats, pantaloons, knickerbockers and bloomers, but the majority of skirt-clad bare arses, not excluding that of his very own sister?'

His eyebrows shot skyward and he adopted a stance as if violated by a vegetable of some not insignificant size.

'You what?!'

'What do you mean, "You what?"' I snorted. 'It's right here in your bundle, adjacent to the internet-data traffic concerning your client's regular visits to BritishUpskirt-PantyPerverts.com. Now tell me, sir, does your client identify as a 'British upskirt panty pervert', or does he profess to be of a more international bent?'

With eyes like saucers he said:

'Hold the judge off for a minute will you, mate? I am shooting down to the cells for a quick conference. This might not be a trial after all.'

## Captain Thor

It has always been a curiosity to me how people can choose to be called whatever they like. One day they might decide to be Nicholas Cooper, the next day, John Smith, without reproach. It would certainly ease the potential for confusion if people were made to stick to the same name, a confusion sadly exploited by our friends within the criminal fraternity.

I recall a young client of mine who was once stopped in a stolen car in the centre of Romford, Essex.

'What is your name, son?' asked the police officer.

'Um… er, Jon?' came the reply, after some desperate and vacuous rumination.

'Yeah? Jon what?'

'Er… um… er… Romford?'

Would it really have been beyond the agency of the local constabulary to have taken young 'Jon Romford' down to the police station, in Romford, seated him and said something like, 'Look, mate, come on!' and possibly even chucked him in a cell for a couple of hours to reflect on his ludicrous assertion?

Instead, I was the one who had to traverse a packed foyer at Romford Magistrates Court one miserable Wednesday morning calling out to a bewildered audience, and thus interrupting Jeremy Kyle on the big TV:

'Is Romford here? Romford? Anyone know Romford?'

It was at least warming to be met with a good Samaritan amongst the villainy seated there who genuinely wanted to help.

'Try the A11, you twat!'

Even Mr Romford himself sat for five minutes or so looking baffled before a lightbulb moment caused his hand to be lifted into the air and our frosty introductions commenced.

It was with the painful memory of 'Jon Romford' still in mind that I gratefully received instructions from a new client, 'The Captain'.

Despite my nomenclative aversions, the irony of the apparent honour implicit in the title 'Captain', as my client was addressed by the Judge, tickled me. This was especially so considering that he was answering charges of masquerading as 'Captain Thor' and pronging a copper up the arse with a barbecue fork. I would even suggest that, such was the almost bizarre feel to the court process – as if of mutiny or an act of cowardly insubordination against the brave captain – the judge felt obliged to adopt a penitent tone when he announced his sentence.

'I am very sorry, Captain, really, very sorry, but I have no choice but to send you to prison for six months.'

Captain Thor, despite the pomp and fanfare, was about as much 'Captain' as my pet cat, Pepper. He was, in truth, a homeless gentleman, formerly Ronald Spiggins from Aston, or some such character, before his alcohol and drug-infused mind exalted him to the mighty hammer-wielding god of Nordic mythology. His unkempt beard, toga fashioned from an old pair of curtains, and a three-pronged barbecue fork lashed to a runner-bean cane completed the look. Granted, there were cues from the Roman god of water and the seas, Neptune, and a possible conflation of myths and theologies, but in times of austerity, when hammers sufficient to create thunder and storms don't come cheap, one just has to make do with whatever godly weapons one can lay one's hands on, from Poundstretcher or wherever else.

Had 'Captain Thor' not alluded to his unworldly power in the Salvation Army charity shop and instead paid the very competitive two pounds asked for the trilby hat, he would surely not have found himself at the raw end of the law. My sympathy for his argument in court that the 'bladed article', was just part of his costume was robustly challenged by the judge who drew some emphasis to the fact that, following one hell of a 'to-do', the barbecue fork ultimately pierced police constable Matthew's anus with some vigour. Police constables should be able to walk the streets confidently and in comfort, it was observed, not have to hop around on them in a manner worthy of the lead performance in Michael Flatley's *Riverdance*.

# No Other Idiot Will
# Do It, So I Guess I Will

Having recently moved to a very reputable and leading set of chambers in the Midlands, I started out as a bit of a bottom-feeder, in every sense of the word. Dining out on the waste products of others was the precondition for receiving the next brief, in this case, a ten-defendant drugs conspiracy.

The case had already done the rounds in chambers and been universally shunned by the popular and hard-working members before it was offered to me as an option of last resort. The reason for its unpopularity was that, whilst it would be relatively lucrative, there were just two months to go before the trial date and close to a million pages of evidence. A case of such mind-boggling complexity would normally take a team of barristers six months to prepare for, working exclusively on it. A single barrister with just two months had not a hope in hell of achieving anything meaningful. I wasn't even a barrister who had two months free. I had a daily list of crap at Wolverhampton Crown Court so long that there wasn't time for a fart, let alone for any genuine preparation.

The previous two barristers who had been instructed many months before had both made excuses and dumped the case, the suspicion being for want of preparation, and in the absence of any possibility that the case would be adjourned, necessity demanded that somebody with a death wish, and an ability to talk himself out of grave trouble, should take on the mantle. I suspect that had cases continued to be remunerated in proportion to their size, then the clerks would have had a larger pool of candidates from which to draw. Seeing as this case, which concerned kilogram-weights of cocaine and heroin all around the country, now paid the same daily rate as one that might concern the selling of a gram of cannabis by Jimmy to his friend, the only name that was up in lights was mine.

Of course, being the greatest conmen of all, the clerks never give you the full picture during the allocation pitch. It is only via determined interrogation that the true extent of the shittiness may be revealed. In the same way as you don't buy a horse advertised as a 'forward ride', 'keen, but not for novices' or 'a bit tizzy' because the thing will be a psychopath that will try to kill you, neither do you welcome a brief euphemistically described as 'challenging' but 'a good gig', 'a good earner', 'straightforward' or with the promise that ' if you do this favour for the solicitors, they will give you lots more work'.

Having conducted all the usual checks, tried all the usual treasons, stratagems and spoiling tactics to avoid it, and knowing for a fact that acquiescence in the gig was on a par with putting my head into a bear trap along with an invitation that somebody kick the trigger, mental-health issues and impecuniosity sealed the deal. The clerks called the solicitors to break the happy news that the long hunt for an agreeable barrister was over, and then delivered the final punch to the kidneys: the revelation that the case would be in Swansea and last for ten weeks!

As you know, I wasn't a great fan of 'city breaks' and had become even less enthusiastic about them the older and more weary I got. Slinging a bag in the van with four boxes of lever-arch files, a couple of suits and a traditionally insufficient number of pairs of pants and socks to last the week, I wasn't exactly filled with the joys of spring as I made my way to Wales.

Neither was my dysthymia displaced by the extravagance of my forty-pounds-per-night seafront accommodation that greeted me on my arrival. The perpetual aroma of stewing cabbage, mesmerising carpet tiles, a wood-veneered cigarette machine, the bar complete with thatched roof and ship's bell, plus other notable features, all combined to create a deeper hell than the sum of its parts.

Not that it was all bad. After being buzzed through the glass security doors, on account of not looking 'too stoned', I scored an upgrade to a room boasting the highly coveted accoutrements of wallpaper, albeit peeling woodchip wallpaper and a sea view – not that you could see the sea, as the windows hadn't been cleaned for perhaps thirty years. It also had a sink, which was ideal as the nearest communal washroom offering alternative facilities for that 3.00am pee was on the landing below.

The court case, at least, was slightly more edifying and, against the odds, it proceeded relatively efficiently. I had listened intently to the prosecution opening speech, which was as much of a revelation to me as it was to the jury, and, with some genuine hard work in collaboration with the solicitors, I attained a working knowledge of the case and something approaching competency. My nightly rest, on the other hand, was considerably less satisfactory.

Every day I would show up to court knackered out of my mind owing to the nocturnal rambunctiousness that reigned at my 'hotel'. Having reasoned pretty quickly that locking oneself in one's room tended to increase one's life expectancy of an evening, insomnia was less easily dodged than death.

Two weeks in and my misery plumbed new depths after a neighbour and his girlfriend set about each other at 1.30am, apparently over the divisive topic of whose turn it was to buy the drugs. By 5.00am. I couldn't take any more and, in a state of sleep-deprived sheer recklessness, I decided to approach the source of the clamour with a conciliatory invitation to desist. I had barely had a chance to open the door before a bald-headed mountain of a man, distinctive if nothing else for his extensive facial tattoos, bounded past me up the stairs, fingers of one hand curled into a fist and a three-foot machete in the other. It was with some purpose that he advanced towards the source of the rumpus, held the machete to his throat and politely counselled him to reduce the volume, warning that failure to do so would 'see his fucking throat cut'.

Whilst certain pillars of society may at that point have called the police, at 5.00am, having missed out on a night's sleep because of this turd, one of those pillars I was not. Nobody could deny that the peace negotiations had lacked a certain 'finesse', but neither could it be said that blissful silence had not been restored owing to this discerning panoply of unpleasantness.

I think I have said it before, that, as a barrister, there is a professional line that should never be crossed when it comes to those of the criminal fraternity; the underworld should be kept at arm's length. This was no time for principles or policy. The only reason I was in this madhouse in the first place was because of the principle- and policy-makers' refusal to pay for anything approaching reasonable accommodation. With that very much in mind, and overwhelmed with gratitude, I gripped this maniac, laid my head on his chest and cuddled him more lovingly than anyone I had ever cuddled before.

Tranquillity restored, I was intent on exploring the surrounding environment in the following weeks. I had rather hoped that the young and good-looking solicitor's representative who had come down from London to work with me for a few days would accompany me to the venerated 'Mumbles Mile' of pubs and bars along the Swansea seafront. Here, with misty-eyed nostalgia for the nineties, we could again attempt to drink twenty pints without shitting ourselves and being taken home in an ambulance, a feat that had hitherto evaded me.

The youngsters of today, sadly, appear to be infinitely more reserved, this one deciding instead to shun the old Lothario in favour of bright eyes and a bushy tail for the following day in court. The toothless proprietor of my lodgings, therefore, was nominated as my best pal, mascot and confidant for the lonely nights ahead until Tinder orchestrated a partnership with a charitable soul from the Port Talbot steel works, complete with shocking pink hair and a motorcycle. With her local knowledge of the Gower Peninsula, the sweetest personality of anyone I had ever met, and with the odd diversion up 'petticoat lane', we explored the coast, making for some truly happy weeks.

Maybe it was the additional sleep I was getting, but whatever the cause, I was able to persuade the jury that my client had not been on multiple drug runs at all, but merely fishing off the beach adjacent to the centre of drug trafficking in the North. The nine other co-defendants were all convicted, including defendant number three, question-ably of unsound mind, who as part of his defence alluded to his possession and use of an 'invisible sex cloak'. None of us knew exactly what an invisible sex cloak was, its relevance, how it worked, or where one might be purchased, but, from the description, we all assumed that it was something pretty cool for which there must be a market.

I have made something in this book of the asininity of your average jury. The question of the collective cerebral agility of these twelve flowed not from their acquittal of my client – there were a number of imponderables which could reasonably have swayed them in favour of the defence – but rather from a question posed to the judge after ten weeks of hearing the case and when the jurors were well into their retirement to consider their verdict. Their note read:

'We have verdicts upon which we are all agreed on ten of the twelve defendants. We are split in respect of the remaining two. Could Your Honour remind us of the names of these defendants, possibly even with the help of a seating plan? We anticipate that we are close to verdicts.'

In a complete state of panic the barristers and the judge all turned towards the dock so as to count the number of defendants twice and three times over, concerned that a terrible and fundamental oversight had somehow occurred. In the end, the judge worked it out. In the preceding ten weeks the jury had not only tried the ten defendants on serious drug charges, but also the two innocent security guards who had accompanied them into the dock. The terrifying part of it all was that the contents of the note indicated that, at the very least, three jurors were of a mind that the security guards were guilty!

# Is This the End
# Or Just the Beginning?

I think I may have said it before that life is much like a marrow. The minute you think you've got both hands firmly on it, it somehow ends up wedged up your arse. The hand behind the vegetable this time, be he bat-eater, bat-shagger or mad scientist, was the bastard who unleashed Covid-19.

I am sure that my professional aspirations mirror those of my friends and associates at the criminal Bar. They don't include lofty ideas of judicial postings in the High Court or wearing silk; they are instead limited simply to survival for the next hour, emotionally, financially and professionally. My inherent and eternal sense of foreboding that the next call, email or court hearing will be the prenuptials to holy matrimony between me and the dung heap, has seldom proved misplaced.

When the Covid-19 hit, the rug was pulled away from beneath all of us at the criminal Bar. Courtroom practice, being fundamentally theatre, for the same reasons as theatres, had to shut down. We couldn't have the saliva-ejaculating pontifications of barristers projected over twelve strangers huddled together in close proximity.

Desperate for ways to reboot the system in the latter stages of the first lockdown, trials began to reconvene with the use of multiple courtrooms to allow the space for 'social distancing'. But with this additional space filched from a system already crippled by a lack of court availability, a situation that many thought couldn't get any worse, got worse.

The latter introduction of Perspex screens to courtrooms, which enclose the jury, the judge, and barristers in individual boxes, provide great opportunities to inadvertently bang one's head, and to muffle their voice when they shout out the words 'fuck it', but probably achieve little else...

In addition to these measures, we have also seen the introduction of emergency 'Nightingale' courts set up in theatres and hotels with a view to keeping everybody safe while at the same time attempting to tackle the dizzying increase in an already challenging backlog of cases. These are a good idea – let's give credit where credit is due. When those in power are criticised for their handling of the pandemic, when people argue that there is the absence of a steady hand on the tiller, that stewardship has given way to buffoonery, that those in control are improvident with our health and money, they might like to have a look at one of the new flagship 'Nightingale' courts and award some points at least:

a.  For finding a venue with enough space for social distancing of the jury. (1 point)
b.  For finding a venue with sufficient space for the barristers and court staff to observe social distancing. (1 point)
c.  For finding a venue where other members of the public may be deterred from visiting to prevent unnecessary interaction. (1 point)
d.  For finding a venue which is inexpensive and therefore provides value-for-money for the taxpayer, such as a hotel which no one else is currently using. (1 point)
e.  For choosing as a venue a Covid isolation hotel, which, by its definition is designed to keep those who potentially have coronavirus separate from anybody else lest it is passed on, which would be even more regrettable if those catching it did so through honouring a public duty. (Minus 40,000 points.)

<u>RESULT</u> : The cynics are entirely justified. Trophy of corpulent twattery fairly awarded, no further adjudications required.

But every silver lining has a cloud, they say, and if any real silver lining could be identified amongst all of this mess, it was the introduction of video court hearings.

In the rush to get going, many court centres adopted pre-existing, commercially available, video-conferencing software which worked really well. The Ministry of Justice, being the Ministry of Justice, not content to utilise someone else's ruggedly tested and expensively developed design, decided to reinvent the wheel, doubtless at eye-watering cost to the taxpayer. The result has been that which goes by the name of CVP (Court Video Platform, or Complete Vaginal Prolapse to its friends).

Although improving all the time, early CVP ensured that you could not be seen or heard by anyone in the courtroom into which you 'linked', neither could you see or hear anything that was going on yourself, except maybe a frozen image or two of a judge or defendant. Leaving those minor critiques aside, on the occasions when video-conferencing technology does actually work, it means that you can sit in your pants in the front room and do the same work as you would have done in person, but without having had to travel for three hours, park, and hang about in court for ages waiting for the hearing. For this reason, the concept gets a heartfelt thumbs up from me.

And it is in pursuit of the felicitous articulation of justice that I do the same thing everyone else does in preparation for the hearing. I sweep all of the clutter away from the eye of my laptop camera, sit in front of a bookcase with a few choice works of literature I have never read and then relax in the knowledge that the judge remains ignorant of the Superman underpants, pineapple socks planted into Christmas Grinch slippers and a sitting room redolent of a crack addict's toilet.

This isn't to say that embracing the brave new world of digital technology is without its challenges. My mind turns to my old mate Hugo, who, when appearing over the link one morning, awarded the honourable judge's obstinacy with an emphatic display of his middle finger when his back was turned, unbeknown to him that witnesses in the case, their families, the local newspaper journalist and representatives of the Ministry of Justice had also linked in to watch the case. It is said that when the penny dropped, on account of the excitable gestures of the court clerk, rigor mortis immediately gripped poor Hugo, instantaneously rendering him stiffer than the stiffest stiffy. What with his fixed stare through the lens of the camera and apparent insensibility to his surroundings, were it not for his trembling fingers fumbling with his tie, it might have been considered that his spirit had bypassed the animation of his limbs and permanently flatulated away; which reminds me, I still need to ask him how the disciplinary proceedings went.

As you may expect, the robing rooms are abound with stories of barristers having similar disasters. My own experience of hitting the skids with this thing may be considered no less notorious. I refer to the occasion when the flexibility of online working was exploited for a business-like evacuation of the bowels.

Distracted by my activity and the concomitant perusal of 'smut' on my tablet, I had all but missed the email that popped up from the court clerk telling me that my case had been advanced up the list and could I join the hearing forthwith? Without the opportunity, or, in truth, the inclination, to truncate my treasured potty time, I considered that little harm could be occasioned by my participation in situ. After all, there would be no reason for the court to suspect that any multi-tasking was going on.

The Judge was of the formidable type, of an ilk which has little regard for the whims and fancies of counsel. Personally, I quite like the bloke, but generally he is despised at the Bar for being as harsh a judge as you could wave a shitty stick at. He would send your client to prison – without fail; it didn't matter what your client had done, nor what you had pleaded on his behalf. It was for this reason that as he passed a sentence of immediate imprisonment on my man, and for some length of time, that I saw some irony in the coincidence of my 'toiletry toiling' with His Honour's disagreeable decree.

And I would have got away with it had it not been for the solicitor-cum-comedian sat in the second row of the well of the court. It was at the conclusion of the hearing, when I'd decided that having a dump while simultaneously participating in a court hearing was a thoroughly agreeable way of doing business, that the bastard pointed at the screen, which from my vantage point was not unlike staring down the barrel of a gun, and exclaimed, 'Hoarder!'

A quick glance behind me confirmed my online backdrop: the lid of a toilet cistern and about twenty bog rolls that rose above it like the Eiffel Tower. The camera switched to the judge, then the clerk, and then to prosecution counsel who all shook their heads regretfully. I bowed my own in shame. It wasn't the shitting in answer to His Honour's peroration that was the problem; it was my stashing of bog rolls during a global crisis that brought scandal on the profession.

A fan as I am of the virtual trajectory on which the criminal justice system is now embarked, the optimism I feel that a healthy criminal justice system is not a prospect entirely beyond reach is based entirely on the continued and ever-dependable magnanimity of all those committed to working within it, whether jurors, giving up their precious time; the lawyers; or the admin staff in the back offices. My gratitude extends even to the technicians who change the many light-bulbs around the mirrors in the dressing rooms-cum-judges' chambers, without whom other incentives for judges to sit in theatres recommissioned as courts would need to be found!

When all is said and done, the overarching reality is that the criminal-justice system still finds itself in an awful mess. There is now a backlog of thousands upon thousands of cases, meaning that justice, and all the associated protec-tions which it affords, continues to be threatened. Criminal barristers have never been objects of public sympathy; the image of the 'fat-cat lawyer' is one that is hard to displace, and is certainly one that populist governments have little interest in correcting. Years of cuts and under-investment have led to a complete lack of new blood in the profession, while a demoralised workforce continues to toil at the coalface out of a sense of duty and honour, all the while managing, just about, on an overdraft.

To make things worse, many barristers have been unable to survive the time out of work during the lockdowns and have left never to return. Those of us who have remained represent a significantly depleted force who sacrifice everything to commit ninety hours a week to work as the whip is cracked to catch up lost ground. And still that isn't enough. Victims and defendants are deprived justice as they wait years for their cases to be heard, cases collapse as witnesses become completely disillusioned, and the message is sent to would be criminals that our criminal justice system is no longer the force to be reckoned with it once was.

From my own point of view, there is much I am grateful for. Restarting the wheels of my trade again has at least saved me from having to sell more items of my property or weld steel lintels at a building site of an evening just to stay afloat. For now.

It was renowned psychiatrist Ronald Laing who perspicaciously said, 'Insanity is a sane reaction to an insane world'. It is an observation to which I suspect we could all relate, nobody more so than those who have the privilege to tread the boards of the courtroom. But with life comes knowledge, and with knowledge comes solace. The keepy-uppy football competitions in the park with my son, the intellectual chats with Pepsi the street cat and, not least, a shrewder approach to meeting people who offer the prospect of genuineness, all contribute to the sunshine that now lift my days.

When my therapist suggested that a tortured mind might be assuaged somewhat by journaling, she was doubtless not expecting a copy of *Dirty Briefs* to be tossed onto her table. Maybe it answers some of her questions.

And now for you, ladies and gentlemen, please never forget: when you find yourself standing by a broken shop window with a jemmy in your hand, or if you have been caught romancing your neighbours' alpaca, come down and see me. For a modest fee, you might just find your saviour.

# Acknowledgements

A huge thank you to David Daniel, David Luxton, and my talented publisher Jo Sollis, whose drive and sense of humour made a dream a reality. Thank you as well to my friends who listened to my stories in the pub and said 'you should put that shit in a book mate, I'd read it', without whom I never would have done so.